WRITE THAT NOVEL!

NIGHTSKY PRESS

Also by
KAREN McQUESTION

FOR YOUNGER READERS

CeliaandtheFairies
SecretsoftheMagic Ring
Grimm House

FOR OLDER READERS

Favorite
Life on Hold
From a Distant Star

Edgewood Series

Edgewood
Wanderlust
Absolution

FOR ADULTS

A Scattered Life
Easily Amused
The Long Way Home
Hello Love

WRITE THAT NOVEL!

YOU KNOW YOU WANT TO...

Karen McQuestion

NIGHTSKY PRESS

NIGHTSKY PRESS

Cover design by www.ebooklaunch.com

Novel component diagram design by Maria McQuestion

ISBN-13: 978-0692671924
ISBN-10: 0692671927

Printed in the United States of America

If there's a book that you want to read, but it hasn't been written yet, then you must write it.

— Toni Morrison

Contents

Introduction

ey there.

Yes, I'm talking to *you*. The one who's been thinking of writing a novel for what seems like forever. You have ideas—really great ideas. They pop into your head at the oddest times; they haunt your dreams. There are times you've imagined the plot points of an entire book from beginning to end.

You read a lot, so you definitely know your way around a story. No doubt about that. Some of the novels you've read are so good they surpass anything you can ever imagine writing. But honestly? So many of them are marginal. Not even worth reading. You know you can do better than those dreadful books. And yet, you don't. You're walking around on planet Earth, a secret novelist who's never written a book.

Time's a wastin', and you're not getting any younger. Not only that, but just in case you didn't know—none of us is guaranteed a good long life. We all imagine dying in our warm, comfortable beds the night after blowing out a hundred candles on our birthday cake. You can't see me, but I'm sadly shaking my head right now. Most of us are completely delusional when it comes to thinking about our own deaths. The truth is that you, me, the guy standing next to you in line at the store— any one of us might have some tragedy befall us at any time, and then BAM! It's all over. A bit morbid, I know, but I'm trying to drive a point home. If you're going to write that novel someday, then someday is here. If you've been waiting for a sign, wait no longer. The universe is tapping you on the shoulder. Tag! You're it.

I know about your secret desire because I was in your shoes for a long, long time. For ages I knew I was born to be a novelist, even when I hadn't written a book. Over the years I had my share of jobs, none of them having to do with writing. My coworkers at the mortgage company, department store, restaurant, and payroll office had no idea they had an undercover storyteller in their midst. All they knew was that my tendency to daydream made me terrible at what I did. I got by on my earnestness. I think they sensed I was really trying. Plus, I always showed up on time and almost never called in sick, which counts for a lot.

I drifted along in life, thinking about writing. (I thought about it a lot, actually, for what that's worth.) Somewhere in there I got married and had three kids. When the youngest was in preschool, I decided I'd had enough. I was ready to come out of my pretend-novelist cocoon and become an actual writer.

That was eighteen years ago. Since then, I've written more than a dozen books, and I'm still going strong. I hope I live long enough to write all the books taking up space in my head, dying to come out.

Recently, Amazon Publishing informed me that I've sold over a million books in total. A million books. Unbelievable. Do I deserve this spate of good fortune? Probably not, but I'll take it anyway. I'd love to run into someone I worked with at the payroll office back in the day so I can tell them I morphed from a not-so-great payroll clerk to a successful novelist. It would be my chance to redeem myself, to prove I'm not so stupid after all. It hasn't happened yet, and it probably never will, but if it does, I'm ready.

Even though a million is an incredible number of sales, so is a hundred thousand, or a thousand, or fifty for that matter. Back when I thought I'd never get published, the idea of fifty people paying to read one of my books seemed pretty farfetched. Two days after I uploaded two books to Kindle back in July 2009 and saw that I had *four* sales, I was overjoyed. No one besides my husband knew they were on the Amazon site, so these sales came from strangers. At the time, the number four seemed like a miracle.

My books are now available in audio, ebook, and print, and they have been translated into four languages. It didn't happen overnight. I worked hard, but I also benefitted from great timing and a lot of luck. I owe a lot of my success to the kindness of readers who helped spread the word about my books. And I can't underestimate the value of my partnership with Amazon Publishing. I wrote the books, but their marketing power surpassed anything I could have done on my own. I am grateful and never take any of it for granted.

When I started out I had no idea how to write a novel, so in preparation I read dozens of books and articles online. I attended workshops, readings, and classes, and all of them were helpful, but each one only offered a bit of pertinent advice. And none of them addressed the practicalities of what it actually took to craft a really great story, one that would keep readers interested and turning pages, eager to read on.

I took in everything I could, gleaning what was most helpful, and then I plunged forth, writing from the heart, hoping that if I cared about the characters and events in my stories, readers would too. As it turned out, I did a lot of things right—some by instinct and some accidentally—but I also made plenty of errors along the way.

I don't pretend to have all the answers. There is no one way to write a novel, and it might turn out that my way might not be your way. Still, I'd like to share what I've learned. Over time I've discovered strategies and learned concepts I hadn't previously encountered in writing books. If I had known these things at the start, it would have made writing easier and far more joyful.

I've written this book as part writing memoir, part novel-writing tips. If you're not interested in how I got from there to here, feel free to skip over the first part, my personal journey. I always enjoy hearing about other writers' experiences, but if you don't, my feelings won't be hurt. Just brush past my years of suffering and heartache like it all counted for nothing and go right to the part that will benefit you.

My hope in writing this book is to help you avoid making my mistakes, and also to share the things I've found helpful. And for those of you who haven't written word one yet, I hope this gives you the impetus to get started.

You can do it. Honest.

CHAPTER 1

In the Beginning

I've wanted to be an author since I was a student in Mrs. DiFrances's third grade class at St. Joseph's Elementary in Wauwatosa, Wisconsin. The turning point came when we were assigned a writing assignment, a short story.

When it came time for Mrs. DiFrances to return our graded stories, she announced that first she wanted to read one of them out loud. I was in complete shock when I realized it was my story and that the class was responding: leaning forward in their seats, laughing at the funny parts, gasping at the surprising plot twist. Something clicked in my brain then, probably akin to what addicts feel the first time they get a rush.

When she told the class I was the writer and that she thought it was excellent, the other kids turned around in their seats to gape at me. I was the shy kid, the klutzy one who wasn't good in gym. I was not anyone you'd notice. But I could do this; I could take something out of my head, put it on paper, and get other people to respond to it.

That's all it took. I was hooked.

In talking to writers, I've found that a lot of them got the writing bug in third or fourth grade. I think that time period is relevant because that's when kids really start reading text-heavy books, and it's also when teachers assign stories. Kids who love reading usually take to writing, and when they're recognized for it, it spurs them on to do more.

From that point on, I became what I call a good student writer. I wrote a little at home, but most of my writing was done at school. Whenever teachers would assign papers or stories, other kids would groan, but I was delighted. It was easy for me—unlike, say, gym, math, or German.

(Just a little side note here: I understand the emphasis on math and science in today's curriculum, but I think the educational system vastly underestimates the value of writing. Being able to express yourself in a clear, concise manner is important. Most jobs require some documentation or writing of reports. Being able to communicate well should be a priority.)

After high school I attended the local university, commuting first from my parents' house and then from an apartment I shared with a roommate. I wanted to be a writer, but there wasn't a novel-writing program and nothing else appealed to me, so I picked English as my major and just dinked along, taking random classes. My mother suggested—several times, in fact—that I become a nurse, because, "They always need nurses." This is very true, and you know why? Nursing is a difficult profession, requiring some very specific skills and personality traits, none of which I have. Seriously, if you're a nurse, you have my utmost admiration. I am in awe of your abilities.

I'd always been a good student, but attending classes at the university was torture for me. I hated the hour-long bus ride each way, and later, when I had a car, I despised the endless circling around, looking for a place to park. In my memory, I was always parallel parking in tight spaces, going back and forth, back and forth, worried about someone hitting my car, or worse yet, me hitting theirs. After I found a spot for my car, I took note of how long I had before I'd get ticketed, then went from class to class, barely making it on time as I rushed from one building to the next. I didn't know anyone on campus, and there was no chance to get acquainted, so I felt anonymous in the worst possible way. Depressed, I wondered, *What is the point of all this?*

Sitting in classrooms and lecture halls weighed on me, too. Much later I discovered I have a sensitivity to fluorescent lights, but at the time all I knew was that I had trouble concentrating. I have no idea why the lights bothered me more than in high school, but they did. In the evening to pay my bills I worked as a waitress. Sadly, serving food and drink to strangers was the best part of my day. In general it was a miserable time. I always felt like I was on the verge of crying. After two years I dropped out, telling people it was because I couldn't find parking.

From there I worked at various jobs, got married at age twenty-two, and wrote two books in my spare time. The books were middle-grade fiction, both around 120 manuscript pages. One was a mystery involving a set of twins investigating the ongoing theft of money from their uncle's restaurant. (Because what kid doesn't want to read a really good embezzlement tale?) The other story involved a magical book that took the main character on all sorts of adventures. Both books were appallingly bad, full of all sorts of newbie errors, like erratic point-of-view shifts, hackneyed dialogue, and timeline inconsistencies. I had fun writing them, though, and I thought they were fabulous. In my opinion, they were ready to be printed, bound, and sent to libraries and stores worldwide.

I wrote both manuscripts using my super cool electric typewriter and got a friend who worked in an office to make copies for me. (Thanks, Katie!) I found a book in the library that listed the contact information for children's book publishers and sent off the complete manuscript, along with a cover letter and a mailer already set up with the return postage. That's how it was done. Usually it took several months to hear back. Each time I hoped for an acceptance letter, but it never happened. Instead, I'd get the whole thing returned to me, along with a nice rejection letter thanking me for my submission and wishing me well. I always felt my stomach drop when I spotted a package with my own handwriting in the mailbox, but for some reason I was never discouraged. I knew I would just keep trying.

I have to tell you that this kind of confidence was completely out of character for me back then. I had an utter lack of self-esteem, not even trusting my own opinion about most matters. If people disagreed with me, I invariably deferred to their judgment. But when it came to writing, something I kept under wraps for the most part, I felt sure I was meant to do this. I don't know why. I just did.

After both books got rejected multiple times, I got sidetracked by life. My husband, Greg, and I bought a house, he went back to school and finished his degree, and after that we had three kids, adopting two of them and having the third the usual way.

We had no time. Greg's job required long hours. As for me, I adored our kids, but they were like baby birds, constantly demanding nourishment and attention. Their relentless chirping charmed me and also made me a little crazy. They insisted on being fed and clothed and taken care of when they were sick. And then there were baths and stories and trips to the park. On and on it went. I mean, it literally never ended. Like most parents with small children, my wants and needs took second place.

Although that period in my life lacked any writing on my part, one interesting thing did happen. My husband, whose degree is in computer engineering, bought a computer shortly after he went back to school. I can't even tell you how unusual this was back then. Friends would say, "You have a *home* computer?" in the same way you'd wonder at someone owning their own centrifuge or hyperbaric oxygen chamber. Every two years Greg would get a new computer because the old one was outdated, something that always killed me because it was a huge financial strain on our budget and I had trouble seeing the benefits.

For me there wasn't much of interest to be found online. Most of the sites were academic in nature, and although Greg set up an email address for me, I didn't know anyone else who had email. It was early days for the Internet, or as it was commonly known at the time, the World Wide Web. One night in the early '90s, after the kids were in bed, Greg showed me a writing forum on CompuServe, and I settled down to read what had been posted. With fascination, I discovered that most of the participants were writing books and were also generously sharing information and tips with each other.

Novelist Diana Gabaldon was one of the forum members. I hadn't yet read *Outlander*, but I could tell by the way the other posters talked about her that she was a big deal. And then I came across one of her posts, asking if anyone knew anything about a type of plant used medicinally during a certain period in history. I can't remember the details, but I know another member popped in and said he knew a professor at a university who was the foremost authority on this kind of thing and he'd connect the professor with Diana. I found this exchange enthralling. I was eavesdropping on people far more accomplished and skilled than myself.

Other posts discussed the idea of varying sentence length to create a sort of musicality to the prose and how to deftly weave in description so as not to bog down the storyline. I read on and on, taking it all in. It was like I'd wandered into a master class on fiction writing and settled into the back row, unnoticed. (The advantage being, of course, that I didn't have to worry about finding parking first.)

If I couldn't manage to write, at least I could read about other people's writing processes. I never posted myself, but at least one or two evenings a week, even though I was tired, I'd sneak downstairs after the kids went to bed and read what was new on the forum. Every now and then Diana would post an excerpt of her work in progress or offer suggestions to other members. I was struck by her generosity. Her words also demystified the whole novel-writing process for me. I watched as Diana Gabaldon created books from the ground up and realized that in addition to being enormously talented, she put in the hours, did the research, and made creating whole fictional worlds sound like fun. It struck me that even though I'd written two books for children, I didn't feel capable enough to create anything longer or deeper.

The conversation on the CompuServe writers' forum helped me to understand that lengthy, complex novels are created step by step. Word by word, scene after scene, each piece building on what came before. I still wasn't entirely sure how Diana Gabaldon worked her magic, but she and the others made it seem doable, which gave me hope that someday I too would be able to create something publishable.

CHAPTER 2

Taking the Leap

Shortly after my younger son entered preschool, I read a listing of community events in the local paper and noticed that a writing group called Chapter One met two Tuesdays a month just blocks from my home. According to the notice, the group welcomed new members.

It took me weeks to work up the nerve to go to one of these meetings. I was very afraid: heart pounding, palms sweating, the whole thing. I desperately wanted to go. I sensed that I needed to go, that it would help me to make connections with other writers and spur me back into the writing mode. At the same time, I feared being exposed as a poser, a no-talent wannabe who was just deluding herself. In my mind, I was meant to be a novelist, end of story, with no backup plan in sight. This worried me, because what if I couldn't get a novel published? What then? If I wasn't a novelist, I didn't know what I was going to do. Going forward might mean going back to square one. But I'd never know unless I tried.

That evening I said good-bye to my husband and kids as if I would be gone for a long time. I grabbed my purse and took a folder, a pen, and a few sheets of blank lined paper. I felt like I couldn't show up empty-handed, but since I hadn't actually written anything in over ten years, I had nothing else to bring. When I arrived at the Hartland Community Center, the door to the room was locked and a piece of paper taped to the glass said the meeting had been moved to the library on the other side of the parking lot. I almost went home. I stood there, sucked in my breath, and decided not to be such an anxiety-ridden idiot, that it was a local group that welcomed new members. It would be fine.

It *was* fine. That night the group consisted of eight people, the youngest being a high school student named Nick and the oldest being the head of the group, a man named John who'd had a historical novel published by a university press. John explained how the group worked. It was basically a writing workshop. The first few minutes of every meeting were spent going over what was new: any acceptances, news of writing contests, interesting articles they'd read, that kind of thing. After that came the critiques. Each writer brought enough copies of his or her work to pass around. The writer would read aloud while the others made notes silently on their own pages. Afterward, they'd discuss the work. In the end, the writers would get their pages back so they could read everyone's notes at home.

We sat around a large table, and John introduced me. The group was friendly, asking what I liked to write, and when I sheepishly admitted I hadn't written anything in a long time but I wanted to get back to it, they nodded in understanding. That night, a woman named Bette brought a craft magazine, which was passed around the table. She'd written an article about rug hooking and taken the accompanying photos, and there, right in the middle of the magazine, were her words and pictures in beautiful, glossy color. I was so impressed. Almost as if reading my mind, someone asked how she'd managed to sell the article. She answered very matter-of-factly, saying something like, "I just submitted it. They had space to fill. I had something to fill the space." It was a simple concept, but I had never thought of it like that before. Publishers need content; writers provide the content. It's a business.

Thus began the first stage of my writing for publication journey. Something stirred inside of me, and I was determined to get published. I felt it would be a sign of validation, giving me credibility as a writer. So much has changed since that time, including my own thoughts on the subject. I no longer believe that someone in an office somewhere has to give a writer a stamp of approval. If you write, you're a writer. Period. But at the time, I felt like I had to justify the time spent away from my family. Getting work published and getting paid for it was my new goal, and I wanted to do it quickly. It seemed like I'd wasted a lot of time already, and I was getting older by the minute.

My mother had a cousin named Peg Dean who'd written for years for a local community newspaper, both as a feature writer and as a columnist. Her column was whimsically titled "Around Peg," and she was well known locally, getting stopped by readers in the grocery store and receiving letters from people saying they found her columns touching and funny. Even though we were related, I'd never met Peg, but Mom gave me her phone number and I gave her a call.

Now I have to tell you that I hate talking on the phone. I have the classic writer's personality: friendly (but not outgoing), easily overwhelmed in groups, and requiring a lot of solitude. And in my case, I'm socially awkward and sometimes afraid of doing something as simple as attending a writers' group or making a phone call. I was determined, though, so I picked up the phone.

Peg couldn't have been nicer. We talked at length about writing, and she told me that the paper used freelance writers to write feature articles for the business and lifestyle section. "The head editor's name is Mary," she said, giving me the woman's phone number. "You can use my name. I'm sure she'll be open to having you do some work for them."

I made a study of the business and lifestyle section, taking note of how the articles were structured. My sister Khris owned her own photography business at the time and belonged to an organization called Wisconsin Women Entrepreneurs. The group had never been featured in this paper, even though Khris said they'd sent several press releases to them over the years.

I decided to write a feature story about the organization, using quotes from Khris and another member, a friend of hers. I figured Mary would be more willing to hire me if I provided a sample of my work. I called Khris's friend and got some information from her, then wrote the article, making sure it was the correct length and written in the style of the others in the paper, and then ran it past the Chapter One group, who suggested a few tweaks. I was ready.

As it turned out, Mary was not thrilled to hear from me. Even after I explained the Peg connection, she didn't warm up to our conversation. "We already have a stable of established freelancers who work for the paper," she said, and I got the impression the matter was closed.

I jumped in before she could say good-bye. "I've written an article I think would be a good fit for your business section. Can I send it to you?"

She sighed. "I guess so. If you want."

I mailed out the story and had almost forgotten about it when Mary called a few weeks later. "I need the contact information for the two sources in your article," she said. "We're sending a photographer out."

"Wait a minute," I said. "You're publishing it?"

"Yes, and I need to reach the two women you quoted," she said impatiently.

I gave her the information and then asked, "So how much will I be paid?"

"Oh." There was a pause. "You were expecting payment?"

"Well, yes. Just what you usually pay your freelancers would be fine."

It was quiet on the other end. Finally she said, "You'll have to fill out some paperwork in order to get a check."

I agreed to that, and once the paperwork was filled out, I became one of the freelancers in their stable. I was assigned to a terrific editor named Sue Sorenson and wound up writing an article a week for the next year and a half. Sue would give me the names and phone numbers of the people I needed to interview and tell me the slant of the article and how long it should be. I usually had anywhere from a few days to two weeks to complete the article. When I was done, I'd email the finished story to her. Rarely did she make changes, except for length.

Subscribing to the paper was a requirement for me. After an article appeared in print, I had to measure the story with a ruler. I was paid $1.75 per column inch. Sue gave me a stack of forms to fill out with the date, headline, and a place to put the column measurement in inches multiplied by the rate, determining how much I would get paid. I'd mail the forms to the newspaper office, and someone there would cut a check, which would be mailed to me. The most I ever made for an article was seventy-four dollars, the least seventeen dollars, but Greg and I were glad to get every penny. It was extra money, and we needed all of it.

Around the same time, I started writing personal essays about my kids and sending them to local parenting magazines around the country. I submitted to multiple markets simultaneously, even though the publication guidelines said not to. Even so, it was slow going, but eventually there were acceptances. Some of the acceptances came after I'd sent out a piece to twenty or more magazines and was nearly ready to give up. These were small publications. A few didn't pay at all or only paid twenty or thirty dollars, but each one was a victory to me. I'd get the clips in the mail and rejoice. Here was proof that something I wrote of my own volition had merit. I mentioned those acceptances in my query letters to larger publications and over time had personal essays published by the *Chicago Tribune*, the *Christian Science Monitor*, the *Denver Post*, and *Newsweek*.

I went faithfully to Chapter One meetings twice a month, and I signed up for other workshops and classes too. I attended author events at my local bookstores. I loved hearing authors talk about how they got their start and how the writing process worked for them.

My friend Vickie had been urging me to read the *Outlander* series for ages, and so I finally did and was blown away by Diana Gabaldon's novels. I came across the passage with the medicinal plant and remembered it being mentioned on the CompuServe message board. I felt like an insider, like Diana was secretly a friend of mine. Only it was such a secret that even she didn't know about it.

And I decided to write a novel, a real novel for grown-ups. I brought parts of it to Chapter One, and the group was enthused, asking where the story was going. I was afraid to tell them I had no idea, so instead I muttered something about it being a work in progress.

"Have you thought of a title?" Nick, the high school student, asked.

I had an idea, but I wasn't sure it was a good one. "I was thinking of calling it *A Scattered Life*," I said.

He nodded. "Cool."

I had about a hundred pages of *A Scattered Life* written when Sue called to tell me that the newspaper budget cuts had eliminated the funds for freelancers. Essentially I was out of a job, but by that time I didn't care. I'd had my fill of writing feature articles. In my mind, I was already on my way to becoming a novelist.

CHAPTER 3

Writing a Novel

In reading authors' blogs, I knew it was common for writers to write multiple books before getting one published. Writing is like any other art—playing a musical instrument, sculpting, painting, composing—you get better with time and practice. The odds were against me. Still, I had a good feeling about *A Scattered Life*. I'd tinkered with it endlessly, moving chapters around, adding backstory, and smoothing out awkward sentences. I knew it wasn't perfect, but it was as perfect as I could make it. My trusted early readers loved it. They said it made them laugh and cry, which I thought was the highest compliment. It was time to look for an agent.

For those not familiar with literary agents, it works very much like it does with real estate agents. They agree to represent your property and don't get paid their percentage until they make a sale. That's where the similarity ends. Literary agents also serve as career advisors and are a conduit for other rights (foreign, movie/television sales, and audio). The idea is that they handle the business details so the writer can just write.

When I completed *A Scattered Life*, going through an agent was the accepted way of having work submitted to the big New York publishers. Having an agent meant you'd arrived, but from what I'd read, getting an agent was nearly impossible. They received thousands of queries a year and wound up representing only a few. Even if you were one of those few, agents usually required writers to revise the book to their specifications, the idea being that they knew what editors were looking for. Many times the offer of representation was contingent upon the writer doing an approved revision of the manuscript.

I've come to believe that some agents ask for rewrites because they like to put their own stamp on the project and also because they want to see how resistant writers are to changing their book. If a writer seems difficult or clueless, this is a red flag. No agent wants to pass on a problem author to an editor. Their livelihood depends upon good relationships with publishers; they aren't going to jeopardize that over an author. Better to take a pass on the book and look elsewhere.

Writers never talked about the downside of having an agent back then. Agents got a percentage of the author's take for the life of the book even if all they ever did was go over a contract once for a few hours. The agency received payment from the publisher, took out their portion, and then cut a check for the writer. This was established, standard procedure, and no one seemed to question it. A good agent could work miracles for an author's career, but it was difficult to tell which agents were good. Very little real information was available about agents besides the deals they'd brokered. From talking to published authors much later I found that the recurring theme was that agents were busy people. Very busy, as important people often are. Brokering high-power deals can be intricate and time-consuming. So what if they didn't answer client phone calls or emails in a timely manner (or at all)? That came with the territory. You were lucky to have an agent. Agents were hard to come by, whereas writers were lined up at the curb, begging for an audience.

Writers would almost never bad-mouth their agents, even after they'd severed ties. The New York publishing world was small, and it was implied that all the agents and editors knew each other. People talked. No one wanted to be branded as difficult. It was hard enough to break into publishing; becoming an outcast wasn't in anyone's best interest.

I didn't know any of that at the time. I'd only read the glowing blog posts of writers who loved their agents. They sent them gifts when the contract went through, dedicated books to them, said they were friends and business partners. They gave them credit for their success, said they'd be nothing without them. There was love all around.

If having an agent was how you got published, I figured I needed to have an agent. As it turned out, over the years I would have dealings with several agents, a mix of men and women, but for the purposes of this book, I'll refer to all of them as "she." I'd prefer not to use their names because my recollection might not match their memory of our dealings, if they remember me at all. In the interest of fairness, I'll identify them by number.

When I was ready to query *A Scattered Life*, I researched agents and agencies, then sent out a first round of fifteen query letters giving details about *A Scattered Life* and listing my writing credits. I'd heard of authors querying a hundred or more agents before finally finding success, so I knew this could be a long process. Usually if an agent was interested in the book she asked to see a partial, three chapters or so. If she liked it, she'd request a full manuscript and give that a look.

Each step took weeks or months, and sometimes you'd send a partial or a full manuscript and never hear back. Complete silence. I had that happen many times over the years. In the beginning I foolishly thought that maybe they'd misplaced my pages or lost my email. A few times I emailed to ask about my submitted manuscript and was told they'd taken a pass. Not getting an answer was considered a no, even if they'd said they'd get back to me.

Writers on message boards compared notes on how long it took for an agent to respond and tried to read meaning into the waiting period. If another writer heard back in five weeks, and the same agent had your full manuscript for eight, it must mean she was seriously considering it, right? Maybe even talking about it at lunch with her editor friends? When the rejection finally came back, the writer took solace in the fact that the agent said she'd love to see future work. That had to mean something, right?

I read those posts and knew my chances were slim, so it was nice to have a few requests for partial manuscripts from my first round of queries. One top-tier agent, via her assistant, requested the full manuscript. I tried not to read too much into it, just printed the pages and mailed them off.

A few weeks later, the agent, hereafter known as Agent One, called. We didn't have caller ID at the time, and I was floored to pick up the phone and find Agent One on the other end of the line. Her assistant had read *A Scattered Life* and liked it. She herself was planning to read it over the weekend but wanted to check first to make sure I hadn't made a commitment to another agent.

Thus began a year of back and forth that ended in heartbreak for me. Agent One thought the book needed some revision, and over the course of the next year we had several phone calls wherein she suggested changes while I frantically took notes, ignoring the sound of my children fighting in the background. I completely rewrote the book twice in that time, once during a two-week writers' residency as a guest of the Ragdale Foundation in Lake Forest, Illinois. After each revision, I dutifully sent the manuscript back to Agent One, hoping it was ready to be sent out to editors.

After the second complete rewrite, she emailed and set up a time for a phone call the following week. Agent One was big on scheduling phone calls, something which made me a little crazy. I never knew if I was getting a call to let me down easy or if it would be good news. This time around I was hoping to hear that the book was finally ready to send out into the publishing world and we'd be discussing a submission strategy.

As it turned out, this call was bad news. She was kind—not that it helped. She said that she and one of her colleagues had read the new version of the manuscript, and both had agreed that, if anything, my rewrite had made the book worse instead of better. Of course, Agent One didn't actually use the word "worse." She was way too professional for that, but her meaning came through. She told me that sometimes it was best to set a book aside and write another one. She said I should keep her in mind for future novels.

I have a history of migraines, and they always start with pressure behind my left eye. As she spoke, I felt that pressure. By the time we hung up, I knew a migraine was headed my way. Coincidentally, it also happened to be trick-or-treat that evening. My older two, Charlie and Maria, were going with a group of friends, while I was planning to take Jack myself. There was no way I could do that now. I called my husband at work and told him he had to come home early to take our younger son out for Halloween. When he arrived home, I put a bowl of candy on the porch and went to bed. The problem was me, I thought. I'd gotten my hopes up. I knew better than that.

I couldn't blame Agent One. She didn't promise me anything; in fact, she'd given the manuscript hours of her time, and now she wouldn't be financially compensated. I was never officially her client. The whole situation had been a speculative venture. I'd failed her, and I'd failed my family too. I'd come close to getting a book represented by an agent and screwed it up.

In retrospect, I've come to the conclusion Agent One and I didn't connect well on the revision notes. She'd say something like, "I think you need to really show *how* they became friends. What was the connection? You could definitely go deeper in that area."

And I'd be thinking that I did show how they became friends, but okay, if it wasn't apparent, I could do more. I'd ask, "Do you want another scene or incident, or should I expand the existing chapter?" and she'd answer that she didn't want to dictate how I resolved the issue, that the impetus for the change should come from me. That it should be organic. Frankly, I didn't know what the hell she wanted, but I tried my best. If I had been more self-confident, I would have been frank with her, which would have given her the chance to elaborate or concede the point. I was afraid, though, of messing the whole thing up, so I nodded and made notes and sort of winged it, which clearly wasn't a good strategy.

Looking back, she was the best of the best as agents go. She was courteous and professional, answered emails and phone calls in a timely manner, and never promised anything she didn't deliver. I didn't fully appreciate her until I realized that her mode of doing things wasn't as common as it should be.

I wasn't ready to give up on the book, so I queried other agents—and publishers too—but there were no takers. The ones who agreed to look at *A Scattered Life* felt it lacked "a great marketing hook." They had a point, as even I had trouble summarizing the plot in a short, catchy way. I finally settled on saying it was a dramedy involving a new wife, her meddling mother-in-law, and her crazy friend. A friendship triangle, I called it, hoping that made it sound intriguing.

Finally I took Agent One's advice and put the manuscript away and started another novel. This time, I vowed, there would be a great marketing hook.

CHAPTER 4

Writing More Novels

My second novel was women's fiction with a dash of danger. This was the premise: my main character, Angie Favorite, is abducted from a strip mall parking lot and dragged up an adjacent wooded hillside. She struggles and is badly beaten but manages to get away. Her attacker is caught and commits suicide in jail. Later, the attacker's mother invites Angie to her house, a creepy old castle, under the guise of apologizing. Angie doesn't want to go at first, but eventually she does and the story goes from there.

I finished the book and gave it a name: *Saving Angie*. I wasn't convinced it was the best title, though, so I also sometimes called it *Finding Angie*. Other times I referred to it by the character's last name, *Favorite*, which is what it ended up being much later.

Favorite had a great marketing hook, I thought. I had a good feeling about this book. I sent it to Agent One, who would have been my first choice. She took a pass. "Just not for me," she said kindly. Argh. *Why not?* I wanted to yell, but instead I thanked her, hung up the phone, and made a list of other possibilities. I queried several dozen agents this time. For months I updated a spreadsheet keeping track of those I'd contacted and what their response had been. When I got a few requests, I sent out the pages and kept my fingers crossed. Finally, one weekend morning, I got a phone call from Agent Two.

Agent Two was really enthusiastic about the book. She was a new agent at an agency primarily known for nonfiction. She would be responsible for the agency branching out into fiction in a bigger way. Agent Two offered representation right away, and before long I had her notes for suggested changes and set to work doing some rewrites.

After Agent Two approved the new version, she made a submission plan, showed me the letter she'd written describing the book, and sent it out to twenty-some editors. I really enjoyed talking to Agent Two. She had zero experience in the agency business—in fact, I think she may have been right out of college—but she was smart and enthused about books and publishing. I Googled the names of the editors who had my novel on their desk, and hoped one of them would love it. I also Googled my agent's name and came across her LiveJournal account. Her postings were professional and gave insights into the life of an agent, something I loved reading about.

As the rejections came in, Agent Two shared them with me, brushing them off by saying, "Oh well, it wasn't for her," or

"She clearly didn't get it." On two different occasions, an editor was interested and took the book to the editorial meeting to pitch as a possible acquisition. Both times I tried not to get my hopes up. Both times I failed. Neither publisher opted to acquire my book. When Agent Two gave me the news, she sounded as disappointed as I felt.

One day as I was reading Agent Two's LiveJournal account, a comment was left by someone who obviously worked with her. I clicked on the name, and it led me back to Agent Two's coworker's account. This woman was not quite as discreet. She talked about problems in the office, everything from temperature control issues to other employees talking too loudly on the phone. One day she casually wrote that she was tired of refereeing the shouting matches between Agent Two and their boss. My mouth dropped open in amazement. *Shouting matches? Really?* I'd worked in my share of jobs, but I couldn't imagine getting into a heated argument with the boss. Was this a New York thing, or what?

By the time all of the editors had rejected my book, the stress in Agent Two's office had reached its peak. I knew this because her LiveJournal buddy said so. Shortly thereafter, Agent Two called to tell me she was going to work at another company, and even though it wasn't a literary agency, I shouldn't worry. She was still going to work as my agent. She believed in the book. Our best bet, she said, was to try some smaller publishers. After she was settled in at the new job, she'd get right on it.

I didn't hear from her after that. Finally after a few weeks of silence, I emailed her and thanked her for her hard work and wished her well in her new job. I said that I thought both of us had moved on and I was no longer going to require her services as an agent. I pushed Send, and a few minutes later the phone rang. It was Agent Two, and the relief in her voice rang clear. She said she'd enjoyed working with me and knew I had a career as a novelist ahead of me. We parted on good terms.

Which was fine, except now I didn't have an agent anymore and the book had been rejected by all the major publishers. It was no longer a fresh new project. *Favorite* had lost its shine. This book wasn't meant to be.

I carefully considered how to increase my odds the next time around. With *Favorite* I'd written a book with a great marketing hook. The problem seemed to be that it didn't fit clearly in any given genre. It wasn't technically a mystery or thriller, although there were elements of both in the storyline. It didn't fit squarely into the women's fiction category. It had some moments of light humor but was far from being comedic. The old woman's castle home had a gothic feel, but it wasn't a gothic or horror novel. I'd created a mishmash of a book.

Next time, I decided, I'd write a book within the guidelines of a specific genre. And if I were going to do that, it made sense to pick a popular genre, one in which editors were actively looking for submissions. By following the deals on the Publishers Marketplace site, I saw that a category called "chick lit" was heating up. Big money advances were being given, and deals were going through quickly. I enjoyed reading chick lit novels, but it wasn't my favorite kind of book. Still, I thought I could write an entertaining story within that genre.

I worked hard on the resulting book, *Easily Amused* and think it's a fun read. The premise is that the main character, a young woman named Lola, inherits a beautiful old house from a great-aunt she wasn't particularly close to. The neighbors are more than welcoming, which doesn't suit Lola, who would rather be left alone. Her old high school buddy Hubert knocks on the door one day asking if he can stay awhile because his girlfriend threw him out of their apartment. Of course the neighbors come to adore Hubert, who fits right in and becomes part of their tribe, much to Lola's consternation.

There are parts of this book which please me to no end. I am especially happy with the depiction of the neighbors. In fact, I wish I could live in that neighborhood. I wrote the story with everything I had, but it was not a book that lit a fire inside me, begging to be written. When I look back, I wish I had been less market-minded and had instead worked on a project that had resonated with me. Of course I'd done that already and it was a complete failure. I felt compelled to be practical.

I was lucky enough to be in a private novel-writing group at that point. I'd taken a workshop at the Redbird Studio in Milwaukee and met three other terrific writers who were also writing novels. We'd get together about once a month and exchange fifty pages at a time, then make notes and discuss the stories. With their help, I stayed on track, completing the book in much less time than it had taken to write either of my previous novels.

When I was all done, it was back to the agent hunt. Of course I checked with Agent One first, but she declined. *Easily Amused* wasn't for her, she said. Then I hopped on the query-go-round and gave it another go. This time, after many months of querying, I was offered representation by a young agent at a prominent literary agency. Agent Three was a few years out of college, had done some good deals, and was seemingly beloved by her clients. With me, she was very straightforward, no small talk, which was fine.

Easily Amused went out to twenty-two editors, and one by one, the rejections came in. One editor at a big publishing house said that although they were not interested in acquiring *Easily Amused*, she liked the writing style and wanted to see what Karen McQuestion would do next. She went on to explain the types of books they were looking for and gave examples of two they'd bought recently.

In a phone call to Agent Three I said, "Do you think we could send her three chapters and an outline of something else?" I'd heard of book deals being done this way and thought it might be good to follow up on this editor's interest right away.

"It's early days for that kind of thinking," Agent Three said. "Let's see what the other editors say first."

As the weeks went by, all of the editors got back to Agent Three with different versions of "no, thank you." *Easily Amused* didn't find a home, and my agent didn't want to send it out for another round. When I asked about the editor who'd expressed interest in future novels, Agent Three brushed it off and said I was better off writing a new novel first.

So I did. The next book I wrote had a teenage protagonist, making it a young adult novel. The title, *Life on Hold*, was my second choice, because the first title, *Waiting for My Real Life to Begin,* had been deemed too long and cumbersome. By now you probably know that I had a good feeling about this book. The young adult market was picking up, and I really felt this one might be the one. Agent Three was not in any hurry to send it out, which made me crazy. First I had to wait for her notes, which took weeks, and then there was another equally long wait after I'd completed the revisions and sent them back. Agent Three seemed decidedly less enthusiastic about this book, but when I asked she assured me she was completely on board and had confidence in the book and in me as a writer.

Finally, finally, the book was sent out to editors, many months after I'd first presented it to Agent Three. The replies were slow in coming, but bit by bit, nice rejections were trickling back. Planning ahead, I started thinking about my next novel. I had several different books in mind, and I wanted advice as to which one would be the most commercially viable. Despite my aversion to the phone, I really felt that this kind of thing lent itself to an actual conversation rather than an email exchange. So I emailed Agent Three asking if she could give me a call when she had a chance. When I didn't hear back, I waited two weeks (because agents are very, very busy) and then left a voice mail with the same request. Two weeks of silence later, I sent another email and two weeks after that, another phone message.

I ran into a writer friend at the grocery store and told her how aggravated I was that my agent wasn't getting back to me. My friend wrote mysteries and was published by one of the big New York publishers, so her experience with agents and editors surpassed mine. "You know this is a thing they do, right?" she said. I had no idea what she was talking about. She went on to explain that an agent is always most enthusiastic about a writer's first book. Then, once it's rejected, the writer and her books have the taint of failure on them. The agent won't drop the writer, because she's already invested time and energy, but that writer is no longer a priority. Other, newer, more exciting projects get fast-tracked while the failed writer has to wait for the down time for anything to happen with her book. "She'll get back to you eventually," she said. "I'd just let it go. You don't want to get your agent mad at you."

A short while later, I was reading through what was, at the time, a roster of blogs I skimmed on a regular basis, when I came across one written by another of Agent Three's clients. The author had referenced Agent Three in past blog posts. They were on very friendly terms, had really hit it off. This was fine with me. Some people you click with, others, not so much. I got that. But this most recent blog post made me sit up and take notice. She and her agent, the author said, had spent all afternoon having an online chat that was the most hilarious conversation ever. And then she posted a screenshot showing part of it, and frankly, it was pretty funny. But I also found it infuriating. Agent Three didn't have ten minutes in nine weeks to talk to me on the phone, but she could spend all afternoon doing this?

I was close to being done before then; now I was really done. I sent an email to Agent Three saying I'd tried getting in touch with her four times in the last two months without success. Clearly I'd overstayed my welcome and I thought it would be best if we parted ways. I thanked her for her time and effort on my behalf and wished her well. Then I cc'd her boss and sent it off. Minutes later, Agent Three emailed back. It was a nice email saying that of course I hadn't overstayed my welcome, but if I wanted to bow out, she understood. And then she reminded me that in an earlier conversation she'd said that our communication would be on an "as-needed basis." Obviously, the "as-needed" only went in one direction.

My husband and I have used those words countless times since then when we're joking around. It fits into more circumstances than you'd think. Anytime I forget to pick up something at the store, I'll remind him that I didn't really forget—

that it was on an as-needed basis. It's the phrase that excuses almost everything.

Once again I no longer had an agent. Agent Three had said she'd let me know when the rest of the responses to the submission came in, but she didn't. When I emailed two months later, she said they'd all said no.

In the meantime, I had the idea of converting *Favorite* into a young adult novel. This required making Angie a teenager. Her ex-husband became her father, her mother became her grandmother, and her son became her brother. I changed it so that her mother had disappeared five years earlier and Angie comes to find out there's a connection between her attacker and her mom's disappearance. It was a crazy rewrite. I wound up scrapping a third of the book, and in the end I had a different, shorter novel.

I queried agents for this new YA version, and one called with interest. We'll call her Agent Four. We talked on the phone for an hour, and Agent Four said she really liked the book but felt it needed some changes. Her assistant went over it and emailed some excellent, helpful notes, and I wrote my heart out for three weeks. I sent the revised manuscript back and waited. A month later, she sent a terse email saying it wasn't for her, thanks anyway. Shortly thereafter, she left the company and joined a different literary agency. I like to think that maybe she got caught up in the new job and didn't have time; I'll never really know.

At this point, I realized I'd lost the joy of writing, the very thing that brought me to novel writing in the first place. Instead of my brain teeming with possibilities, my head was filled with the voices of agents and editors telling me what the market was looking for and why my stories weren't working.

CHAPTER 5

Trying Other Things

Dealing with agents had been exhausting. The ups and downs, the dashed hopes, the never feeling good enough. Some of that was on me, of course. Eleanor Roosevelt was right when she said, "No one can make you feel inferior without your consent." Even knowing that didn't help. I was tired of writing books to other people's specifications without the promise of publication. I didn't want to give anyone that power again. And yet, I wasn't ready to give up completely.

I decided to do two things: start writing for myself again, and seek publication without an agent. The second was necessary because I didn't actually have an agent, but I didn't think of it that way. I'd been the one to cut ties with my last agent. I wasn't fired; I'd quit. Or maybe I'd fired her. Or perhaps she'd ignored me hoping I'd walk away. In any case, I was on my own.

I emailed editors directly. A few actually agreed to take a look, much to my delight and surprise. I queried the new young adult version of *Favorite* to one editor, who asked, "Isn't Agent Three your agent?" She went on to say that she'd just returned *Life on Hold* to Agent Three. The editor apologized profusely, saying she'd only held on to the submission that long because there had been a possible upcoming opening in their publication schedule, one that had never transpired. It had come close, but unfortunately she had to turn my book down. This was weeks after Agent Three had told me that all the editors had gotten back to her.

None of the editors who read my pages offered to buy any of my books, but they were courteous and got back to me fairly quickly. Some of them took the time to tell me what they liked about my stories and what didn't work for them.

One day, I had an idea for a children's book. A little girl named Celia lives in a house in the woods. At the start of the story, Celia's parents tell her that her grandmother, who grew up in that same house, is coming to live with them. Grammy begins telling Celia stories of the fairies she encountered in the woods when she was a child. Her parents tell her Grammy is just spinning tales, that none of it is true. Of course after that the granddaughter meets the fairies and has her own adventures. I happened to mention the idea to my friend Michelle, who said, "Oh, Josie loves fairy stories." Josie was her daughter and my goddaughter. I loved the idea of writing a book for girls her age. I didn't have publication in mind. I just wrote it for fun.

When I finished writing *Celia and the Fairies*, I set it aside, thinking that at some point, if nothing else, I could have copies made at Kinko's and give one to Josie as a present. In the time it took me to write it, she'd aged out of this kind of story, but I thought she'd at least appreciate the thought.

I kept my eyes open for other opportunities in publishing, submitting books to smaller publishers who had an open-door policy and entering my books in contests. *Easily Amused* was a semifinalist in the Amazon Breakthrough Novel Award contest in 2008, but it didn't go any further. Again I was close, just not close enough.

I was still obsessively reading industry blogs and articles about publishing, and taking note of anything that might help me. One morning in July 2009, I came across a short article about an author named Boyd Morrison. Boyd was an agented thriller writer who hadn't been able to break into publishing. A short time after he'd uploaded three unpublished novels to Kindle, they'd garnered over seven thousand downloads and some excellent reviews. Based on this, his agent was able to sell one of the books, *The Ark*, along with a follow-up book to be published in hardcover and audio to Simon & Schuster's Touchstone imprint. It was a six-figure deal, not including the foreign rights deals that were also in the works.

You can do that? I thought. *Upload a manuscript and sell it on Kindle?* In 2009, I knew what a Kindle was, but I had never seen Amazon's new e-reader. At the time, Kindles cost just under $400, and that didn't even cover the books. Frankly, I didn't see the allure. You could buy a lot of books for the cost of a Kindle. For that matter, you could take out books from the library for free.

That was my opinion as a consumer. As an aspiring author, I thought that any possible way to connect my books with readers was great. I looked into it and found out anyone could upload books through what is now KDP (Kindle Direct Publishing) but was then called Amazon's DTP (Digital Text Platform). All I needed was a book, a cover, a description, and a price. They also wanted my bank information so they *could pay me.* Making money from fiction—what a mind-blowing thought.

My husband and I spent an entire weekend uploading two books. Seriously, the whole blasted weekend. DTP accepted plain text and Word documents as well as HTML, but HTML converted most successfully. The problem was that I wasn't familiar with HTML, and Greg only knew the basics. Because he was a computer engineer, I thought he should be a whiz in this area, which shows how much I knew about what he did for a living. For my two test books, I'd chosen *Easily Amused* and a collection of humorous essays that I titled *Lies I Told My Children*, because I knew these two documents were well edited.

The process went like this: We'd upload a manuscript and then review it, only to see that the formatting was wonky—paragraphs not indented, chapter headings off to one side, too much spacing between chapters. To fix those problems, we'd reformat it and upload to review again. Then we'd notice some other problem, and we'd have to do it all over again.

I used photos taken with my digital camera for the book covers. I figured all I'd have to do was add the title and my name, and how hard could that be? I found out. At one point, our daughter, Maria, who was a high school student at the time, walked past as I was cursing up a storm. She stopped to ask what was wrong. "I'm trying to put text on this image, and it's absolutely impossible," I said. "I have tried everything, and nothing works. It's impossible," I added, in case she didn't get it the first time.

She took over and managed to do the impossible in about ten minutes.

By Sunday night, we'd finally figured it all out, just a few minutes shy of filing for divorce. The books still had a few minor spacing issues, but they were as good as we could make them. Greg said, "I hope this is worth it." I hoped so too. It was not one of our better weekends.

By Monday morning I had four sales. Four! Three for *Easily Amused* and one for *Lies I Told My Children*. I couldn't believe it. How did they even find my books? I realized later that getting in early had given me a huge advantage. I'd chosen "romantic comedy" as one of my keywords, not knowing that when Kindle readers used that in a search, *Easily Amused* was one of only seven books that popped up. There were 350,000 books on Kindle at the time, a number that seemed daunting (now there are more than ten times that), but with judicious use of keywords and categories, my books had some visibility. Today if you search for a romantic comedy on Kindle, more than 31,000 results come up. My timing had definitely been good.

Because my books were priced at $0.99 and $1.99, the profit from each sale was small. Still, at the end of July, after ten days, I'd made thirty dollars. Lunch at Applebee's, on me!

The next month I made three hundred dollars, and Greg said, "How many more of these books do you have?" I had to tick them off on my fingers to come up with a number, something I found funny. Over the next few months we uploaded the rest of them: *A Scattered Life*, *Favorite*, *Life on Hold*, and

Celia and the Fairies, giving me a total of six books in all. I almost didn't upload *A Scattered Life* because I associated it with shame and failure. It wasn't until my mother asked about the book, mentioning specific parts of the story and saying how much she liked it, that I considered it. When I went back to the manuscript, the original *pre-agent* manuscript, it read better than I remembered. I went over it one more time, taking out a big chunk of backstory (Agent One had been right about that) and fixing some clunky sentences, and then I put it up on Kindle.

For ten years I'd tried to get a book published, and now people were buying and reading my books. I could not believe my luck. My whole world changed overnight. I was like Dorothy in Oz when everything went from black-and-white to color.

My husband jokingly said, "I guess you just had to wait for them to invent the Kindle."

I wrote an essay about my experience titled "Jeff Bezos Is My Hero," and submitted it to my local NPR station. They invited me to the studio to record it as a guest reader, changing the title to "How We Read Now."

"Otherwise," the producer said, "it will sound like an ad for Amazon."

Good things just kept happening. I started posting on message boards geared for Kindle readers and met some enthusiastic members who talked about why they loved reading ebooks. A visually impaired woman said that when even large print books proved impossible for her to see, she'd mourned, thinking she'd never be able to read again. The Kindle changed this for her, and she was grateful. Another woman said her dyslexic son could read more easily using the Kindle's largest font size because it allowed him to concentrate on one sentence at a time. Others talked about the ease and speed of acquiring books and how handy it was for commuting or traveling. The other authors on the message boards exchanged helpful, encouraging information, with the idea that we were all in this together.

On one of the message boards I connected with an avid reader named Alice L. Kent. She saw the titles of my books listed in the bottom of my signature and said she'd check them out. Alice returned a few days later to tell me she loved *A Scattered Life*, and because we were on a public message board for Kindle readers, others chimed in to say they'd give it a try. From there, Alice read more of my books and talked them up on the message boards. I was delighted and a little embarrassed, hoping that no one would think I'd put her up to it. There was a definite correlation between her word-of-mouth endorsement and the surge in the sales of my books. I call it the "Alice Effect." I give her complete credit for helping get my writing career off the ground. We've kept in touch, and although we've never met in person, I consider her a friend. She's one in a million.

I started following author J. A. Konrath's blog too. Joe Konrath had been traditionally published to great success and was an advocate of self-publishing in Kindle. He himself had uploaded all the unpublished novels he'd written prior to his first sale with Hyperion. He made a great case for writers to use Kindle as a vehicle to reach readers and make money, but he was getting some flak from publishers and traditionally publishers authors, who said his success with ebooks was only because he was an established name.

One day on his blog he said he knew that there were others doing just as well without the benefit of having been traditionally published, and would one of them please speak up and tell his or her story in the comments? I left a comment that evening saying I'd had six books on Kindle for about nine months and had already sold thirty thousand copies with absolutely zero name recognition. I woke up in the middle of the night thinking, *What have I done?*

I'm from Wisconsin. In the Midwest, if you talk yourself up too much, people think you're either lying or bragging. I'm not sure which is worse. If I could have erased my comment right then and there I would have, but it was on Joe's blog, not mine. I felt physically ill and had trouble sleeping the rest of the night. In the morning, I checked Joe's blog and exhaled in relief. The other commenters were supportive and excited for me. No one accused me of lying or being a braggart.

A few weeks later, Joe interviewed me for his blog, which gave me more visibility. From there, the media picked up my story, and I was interviewed for several articles, including one in the *Wall Street Journal.* As a result of that article I got hundreds of emails, many from writers who said their story of trying to get published matched mine. I also heard from a few traditionally published authors who were unhappy with how their books were handled. One said her editor forced her to kill off a main character against her wishes, and another had the opposite problem: his editor insisted that a dramatic death be changed to a miraculous cure. Neither book did well, and the sales numbers were so bad no other publisher would touch them. Hearing my story gave them hope their careers weren't over. They had another option.

I also heard from several literary agents who wanted to know if I was interested in talking about representation. I politely declined. A few years later I was at an industry event and a man introduced himself as being the head of a literary agency. "I don't know if you remember this," he said, "but one of the agents in my office emailed you to see if you'd be interested in working with us, and you emailed back, 'No thanks. I'm good.'" He chuckled at the memory.

I'm guessing they didn't get that kind of response very often.

The head of a small Los Angeles production company contacted me wanting to option *A Scattered Life* for film, and we worked out an agreement. I found out later that many, many books get optioned for film, and almost none of them get even close to becoming a movie, but it was still a thrill. As deals go, it was a tiny one, just a few hundred dollars for the option (like calling dibs on a book). There were clauses in the contract for more money with every step of the process, but it never went any further, and the option eventually expired.

What the option did accomplish, in my case, was to get the attention of Amazon's new publishing company, AmazonEncore. I received an email from senior editor Terry Goodman, who said he wanted to congratulate me on the movie option for *A Scattered Life*. He also said he'd love to talk to me about the possibility of AmazonEncore acquiring the rights for the book. After telling me about the services they could provide for me as an author, he went on to say that with my online and media savvy, the book's reviews, and Amazon's marketing power we'd make a great team. He wrapped it up by saying he hoped to hear from me soon.

Thus began a beautiful partnership. Terry was my editor for eight books before he abandoned me by retiring. I've tried to guilt him into returning, but he's having way too much fun to fall for my nonsense.

I will be the first to admit that I benefitted from timing and luck. The stars aligned just right so that I had a hard drive full of finished novels ready to upload when Kindle came on the scene. I had Alice L. Kent and Joe Konrath and Terry Goodman and many others, including the Amazon marketing team, helping me along. I can take credit for the actual books and the repeat readers, though. Someone in the know once told me that if a reader liked one of my books, the data showed he or she tended to buy and read another, something that thrills me as an author.

In the past few years, many authors who got their start self-publishing in ebook have eclipsed me in numbers and name recognition, and honestly, I couldn't be more delighted for them. I had my day in the sun: appearances on ABC's *World News Now* and *America This Morning*, an interview on NPR, and a mention in *Entertainment Weekly*. Pretty heady stuff for an introvert like me. Believe me, I was glad to step out of the spotlight and get back to writing novels, something I can now do for a living. It's all I've ever wanted, so it's easy for me to be happy for others' success. I subscribe to the notion that there's plenty of room for all of us.

CHAPTER 6

My Process

Beginning writers usually love hearing about an author's process, so I'm including it here. This is not to say that this is the definitive way of writing a novel. The right way is whatever works best for you.

For me this is what works best. Although I work from home, I plan my week as a structured schedule. I write five to six days a week, always aiming for two thousand words. At the start of a book I generally do less than the two thousand words, and at the end, sometimes double or triple that. As I get deeper into the story, the momentum builds and it gets easier to write larger segments in one session.

Before I begin, I take a few minutes to jot down the key points of the scene I'll be writing that day. I do this using pen and paper, old-school style. The notes are just for me, so they would probably be an almost unreadable jumble to other people. I don't write specifics, just the things I want to remember to include: specific turns of events, character reactions, that kind of thing. I'd always done this mentally, but writing it down helps enormously. I started this practice after reading Rachel Aaron's book *2K to 10K: Writing Faster, Writing Better, and Writing More of What You Love.*

When I first started writing, I was lucky to get five hundred words done in a day. Back then I tried to make sure every sentence was perfect before moving on to the next. It was arduous work, and although I loved writing then, I love it more now. My new philosophy, adopted after reading Dean Wesley Smith's blog on the subject, is to write quickly. (Rachel Aaron also recommends this strategy, but I read Mr. Smith's account first.) The idea is that there are two parts to the human brain: the creative side and the critical side. Writing slowly allows the critical side to interfere with the process. And really, who needs that? We get enough criticism from outside sources; we don't need it coming from within.

Writing quickly taps into the creative side and keeps the critical side at bay. Sometimes you hear writers talk about getting into the flow. I find that I get into the flow when I stop thinking about what I'm writing and just write. I focus on getting the words down as fast as possible, knowing I can always revise later if need be, but I can't revise what's not there. Counterintuitively, I've found that the quality of my writing is actually better than when I anguished over every word. Faster, more fun, and better? What's not to like?

If you have difficulty letting go of your perfectionist side, you might want to try Dr. Wicked's *Write or Die* website, found easily through Google. The site is set up with a blank text box, just waiting for you to start typing. You set the time and number of words you'd like to complete, and off you go! If you idle too long, pausing to think or whatever, the site is set up to "punish" you by making annoying noises or (in one setting) erasing what you've already written. You can use it online for free or download it for a nominal cost. I don't use it often, but when I do, it's amazing how I can go from an "I can't write at all" sort of day, to "Wow, I just got a few hundred words done in half an hour, and now I want to continue." Sometimes writing is like exercising. If you can trick yourself into taking a walk around the block, chances are you'll just keep going. It's the getting started that's hard.

If I'm working on a novel, I try not to schedule anything during weekdays if at all possible. When there's a dentist appointment or whatever, I try to work around it.

Each day, I go over the previous day's pages and revise as I see fit. Usually it's just a matter of smoothing out snarled sentences or adding some description. Doing this gets me back into the story. It's the running start that helps me jump into the pool. I've always done this and didn't think much about it, but I've discovered that lots of other authors do it as well. I've heard it called "cycling" and "looping." Whatever you want to call it, it's an effective way to work up to the spot where you left off, making it easier to continue on from there.

I generally write on a laptop (Wi-Fi switched off), sitting in my recliner. Sometimes to mix it up I write longhand in a lined notebook or work at my desktop computer. More recently I've been playing with Dragon NaturallySpeaking dictation software. It's so much fun to talk into the microphone and see the words magically appear on the screen. The end results of a dictation session are lots and lots of words, sometimes as many in an hour as I'd do in a day typing on my keyboard, but I'm still finessing the process. The dictation sessions usually require a ton of revision, and not because the software isn't accurate. It is, remarkably so. The problem is me. I tend to ramble when I dictate, and I also sometimes forget to verbally include the punctuation. The best part about the dictation software is that talking out the story loosens me up. It's a great tool to use when I'm having trouble getting into a story.

I use Microsoft Word and don't divide chapters as separate documents. Each book is one document that I keep adding to. If I want to rearrange text, I cut and paste. I've been toying with the idea of writing a novel using Scrivener writing software. I know many writers who swear by it. They say it's got all sorts of advantages over Word, and they make a good case, but part of me thinks if it's not broken, don't fix it. Maybe someday I'll give it a go.

I don't show anyone the manuscript until I'm completely finished. In the past, I sometimes shared pages from novels while they were still a work in progress and found that it was easy to get derailed by the comments of others. After that I decided if anyone is going to mess up my book, it's going to be me.

The way I write and my ideas about the process evolve and change with time. If you had asked me a few years ago if I thought I'd be interested in trying to dictate a book, I would have answered with a resounding no. Writing fast? Nope, I would have said, not for me. Self-publishing? Never! (I was so close-minded back then.) What I've discovered is that it's fun to try new things, and sometimes it's advantageous as well. Who knows, maybe someday I'll plot out a book ahead of time. Or learn Scrivener and wonder what took me so long. I've learned never to say never.

But enough about me. Let's get back to you. If you want to write a novel, it all starts with a good story, one that readers will want to read and one that keeps them reading. Let's talk about that, okay?

CHAPTER 7

The Making of a Novel

Who should write a novel? Well, you and me and anyone else who wants to. I believe some people are born to write books in the same way some people have a knack for composing music and others have a talent for drawing. It's woven into your creative DNA.

If there's storytelling in your blood, you'll have an easier time of it than most. How do you know if you're a naturally talented writer? Well, you've probably been recognized for your writing ability at some point in your life, most likely at school or work. Ideas come readily to mind. You can make a conversation about what happened over the weekend into an entertaining tale. People rave about your emails or texts or posts. You have a way with words, they say.

For those of you who don't fall into that category, I would still advise you to go for it if that's what you want. I have zero musical talent, but with lessons and a lot of practice, I believe I could become adept at playing a musical instrument. Would someone pay to hear me perform? Maybe not, but why shouldn't I have the fun of doing it, if that's what I want? And who knows, perhaps I've got more talent than I know, or my drive to succeed will compensate for my lack of talent. Never sell yourself short—plenty of others are willing to do that for you.

Practice and determination can surpass innate talent. I've seen it happen. If you want to write a novel and you have the drive, you should do it. I think I have a knack for writing, and as I said earlier, my first two efforts at writing novels, the middle-grade books, were appallingly bad. Honestly, they stunk up the place. With time, I learned and practiced and got better. That's how it works.

Why write a novel? There are many reasons. Some want to create a lasting legacy, something left behind for future generations. Others like the challenge and want to prove they can do it.

The best reason, in my opinion? Because you're driven to tell stories in a big way and want to share them with readers.

The worst reason? Because you think it's a guaranteed way to make money. Excuse me while I suppress a laugh. Here's the truth of the matter: while it's never been easier to get a novel out into the world, that's also true for everyone else, so there's a lot of competition out there. Sadly, some really great books will never get their due. If you're writing for the joy and feeling of satisfaction, you'll still have that at the end of the day even if the book doesn't take off the way you'd like. If it feels like a homework assignment that goes on forever, and then, when you're finally done, no one even buys or reads the book, you're going to feel shortchanged. Or maybe even mad. Certainly you'll feel frustrated and disappointed. Honestly, if money is your primary goal, there are easier ways to earn it.

But let's say that's not your goal. We'll work on the assumption that you're passionate about the written word and have some great ideas you'd love to follow into a novel.

How do you start writing a novel? One word at a time. One page at a time. One chapter at a time. Every author has his or her own methodology, so don't worry; there's no way to mess this up. There's also no way to know if you're doing it the right way because the right way is whatever works for you. Freedom!

Some authors plot out their entire novel and do things I've heard called "character work." Before they even start, they've got the whole book mapped out. They know the physical description of each character, their ages, and personality types. Favorite foods and how they dress. These writers spend hours researching locations and weather and customs. They pin photos of people and buildings that fit their imagined characters and locations. It sounds like a sensible approach, and it might work for you, but my head hurts just thinking about it.

I've tried outlining with the hope it would expedite the process or take away the fear I feel when I reach that spot where *I have no idea what comes next*. What I've learned is that knowing everything ahead of time drains me of my motivation to write. When I don't know what happens next, I experience the joy of discovery, much like I do when I read a book and the wanting-to-know-more spurs me on to continue.

The fear, by the way, is part of the process for me. When I get that knot in my throat, the anxiety of sensing that I've written half a book and it's all a load of midden and I should scrap it and start over, I remember that I always feel that way and it always turns out fine. It was my husband who pointed out the pattern. I guess he got tired of me pacing around the house, lamenting that I had written 150 pages of crap and *what was I thinking?* Writers can be very dramatic at times.

I usually start with a scene. In *Easily Amused*, I knew Lola would be walking down the sidewalk in her neighborhood and encounter a group of her neighbors. When she approaches, they stop talking, giving her the sense that they'd been talking about *her.* What were they saying? She didn't find out until later, and neither did I. One page at a time, we both figured it out.

In my young adult novel *From a Distant Star*, I knew more of how things would transpire before I even began to write the book. I imagined that the dog, Mack, is outside at night, where he witnesses a light fall from the sky and land right next to the barn. Inside the house, I knew Lucas Walker would be dying in a hospital bed in the dining room with his mother and girl-friend nearby. It was certain to me that Lucas would become miraculously cured, and that the two events were connected, but after that I was a little fuzzy on the details.

I often feel like I have a beginning and (happy) ending clearly mapped out in my head, but the in-between part is cloudy. I usually have a few scenes in mind, but nothing is set. Somehow, though, my subconscious comes up with what happens next. One chapter at a time, I build my book. I have to agree with E. L. Doctorow's take on novel writing: "Writing is like driving a car at night in the fog. You can only see as far as your headlights, but you can make the whole trip that way."

Fasten your seatbelts, my friends, it's going to be an exciting ride!

We'll start by talking about the components of a great novel. Or wait, let's ratchet it up a bit and talk about the *perfect* novel. For me, the perfect novel is the combination of three parts: storytelling, language, and emotional connection. You get all three right—a riveting plot, beautiful wording, and a story that taps into the heart of your reader—and you've got yourself a masterpiece. It's a rare thing, and it's also completely subjective. What I consider a perfect novel might not be your perfect novel. Still, I think it's important to break it down and define the novel trifecta.

The perfect novel in diagram form would resemble a triangle consisting of language, storytelling, and the ever-important emotional connection.

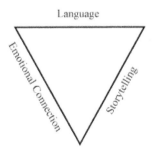

The Three Components of a Perfect Novel

This is what I shoot for every single time I write a novel. Each time I do my very best, and each time, despite my best efforts, I come up short. It reminds me of when I was a kid trying to draw a horse. I could vividly picture the horse. I had my colored pencils sharpened and ready to go. I drew carefully, outlining first, then shading in areas, the way I'd seen other kids do, but despite my best efforts, the picture never turned out the way I imagined. Other people would see my drawing and say, "Great horse!" Of course, they didn't know how I'd envisioned it at the start. They had no idea how disappointed I was with the end result. That's how it is with me and novel writing. Mystery author Rex Kusler once said, "I think my best work is years away," a sentiment I would echo for myself.

It might be that the perfect novel is a myth, a mirage that lets me get closer but always stays out of reach. Luckily, I love to write, so I'm not deterred.

It seems to me that out of the three components of a perfect novel—language, storytelling, and emotional connection—most authors have at least one trouble spot. Maybe their actual writing is marginal, but they tell rip-roaring stories with a lot of heart. Or they tell a heartfelt story with lovely prose, but not much happens. Or the writing is absolutely gorgeous and readers love the twists and turns of the plot, but they feel disconnected from the characters.

Although the goal is always to achieve all three, I've found that readers are most forgiving of language glitches. As long as the story pulls them along and they experience it with the characters, really feeling what they're going through, they tend to overlook typos and clunky sentence construction. This is not to say writers shouldn't take care with grammar, punctuation, and word choice. All of those things are important, of course, but a good editor can help in that area, while it's hard to plump up a flat story.

But I'm getting ahead of myself. Why don't I talk about each side of the triangle and give you some ideas and tips for maximizing your efforts in each area? Okay? Okay.

Moving on!

CHAPTER 8

Language

We'll start with language, my own personal nemesis. Argh. It's the horse I want to draw that turns out to be more primitive than realistic. I read other authors' books with envy and think they're the equivalent of Michelangelo while I'm Grandma Moses at best.

Knowing I don't measure up makes me feel like I shouldn't even bother. And then I think, *Snap out of it—there's nothing wrong with being like Grandma Moses!* After all, she's a renowned American folk artist. People love her nostalgic depictions of simple farm life and rural landscapes. It's just a different style. Not everyone can be like Michelangelo.

But irrationally I want to be Michelangelo, and it frustrates me to know I'm not and never will be. I imagine a voice coming from the clouds saying, "Too bad for you, Karen McQuestion! You must work with the skills you have."

And really, isn't that true for all of us? We all have deficits, and we can either use the knowledge of our shortcomings to work harder, or let it defeat us.

I always struggle with language, but I've gotten much better over the years. Still, my writing style tends to be simple and straightforward. Reviewers never describe my books as having "lush prose" or "evocative imagery." I'm not known for my metaphors or similes (although I thought that horse-drawing thing was pretty good). I have come to terms with the fact that language is not my strong suit, and I work to overcome it.

Happily, readers seem to appreciate other things about my writing. Early in my self-publishing journey I got an email from a reader who said reading one of my books helped her enormously—that it was a few hours of enjoyment during a sad period in her life when she needed a distraction. She thanked me for the first laugh she'd had in months. If I have to be content with something, that's a huge something and I'll gladly claim it.

Basic writing skills come from the correct usage of grammar and punctuation. Very often interviewers will ask authors for the advice they'd give aspiring writers, and the answer will be, "Read a lot and write a lot." Excellent advice, but I'd take it a step further. Read with an eye toward studying the craft. Write with the goal of improving.

I won't go into the specifics of basic grammar and punctuation because that information is readily available elsewhere, and frankly, it's not the most interesting topic. Most likely, if you're a reader, you instinctively have a knack for it. If not, a knowledgeable friend or a writers' group can help you out. There are also some excellent books on this very subject, so if you want to read about subject/verb agreement or dangling participles, you've got lots of options. And if you're not sure of the difference between, say, "awhile" and "a while," or "further" and "farther," help is only a Google search away. Same thing for "lie" and "lay" (something that trips me up on occasion).

I can share a few tips that would have helped me back in the day.

Simplify, Simplify!

Start out by writing sentences that are simple and clear. At writers' workshops I've seen sentences so long and convoluted that by the time I get to the end, I've forgotten how the thing started. If you begin with something basic, you can always expand it later, but it's hard to untangle a sentence once it's become hopelessly snarled.

Another way of simplifying is to eliminate unnecessary words. Very often you can omit words such as: noticed, looked, and seemed. Go through your text once you've finished and see if these kinds of conditional words are necessary. "I noticed he looked tired," is a perfectly fine sentence, but "He looked tired," does the same thing. If the story is told in first person, the reader will assume that the character speaking is the one who notices the tiredness. Same thing with "looked" and "seemed." Tidy up the word clutter and uncover the story beneath.

Along the same lines, you don't have to write, "He nodded his head." Just saying, "He nodded," will suffice. Honest, the reader will assume his head is involved. "She pointed at the cat," is fine. No need to say, "She pointed her finger at the cat." Look for places you can streamline, and your writing will be better for it.

Sentence Structure

Try to vary your sentence length, and when you're done, read your work aloud to hear how it flows. The people on the CompuServe writing forum were right: well-written prose almost has a musicality to it. It's fun, too, to play with sentences, changing the wording, adding words in, taking some out. Try different combinations and see what works best. Eventually, once you're a million words into your writing journey, you'll have to do less of this, but at first it's really helpful. As a writer, you may still be establishing your voice and style, and this is a step on the path.

Mary, Mark, Miles, Milly, Martha

Avoid having characters with similar-sounding names or names that start with the same letter. To you it might be clear, but it's best to eliminate anything that might potentially confuse readers since it will pull them out of the story.

And while we're speaking of names, let's talk about name choice as it pertains to age. If a character is named, say, something like Karen, the reader will assume she's an older woman. (I keep hoping that the popularity of actress Karen Gillan as Amy Pond on *Doctor Who* will bring "Karen" back as a cool name and that suddenly there'll be a slew of baby girls with that name, but it hasn't happened yet.) Names can date your work. If all your female characters are named things like Debbie, Linda, and Patty, and they're teenagers, the story better be taking place in the 1970s or an alternate universe.

Exit Stage Left

Beginning writers often incorporate what I call "stage directions" into their fiction. I've done it myself. It goes something like this: An old lady named Maude sits in a recliner watching TV, drinking a glass of red wine. There's a knock at the door. She sets down the glass and picks up the remote to mute the sound, then gingerly grabs the lever on the side of the chair to lower the footrest before getting to her feet. She rises ever so slowly and shuffles across the room to head toward the door, one step at a time. When she gets her nose right up to the surface, she stands on her tippy-toes and narrows her eyes to peer through the peephole.

Ack! I'm smacking myself on the forehead. What a horrible bit of fiction. Is the fact that she's in a recliner important? If not, you can eliminate the whole lever and footrest business. (Maybe you should take it out anyway—it screams awkward writing.) Does the reader need to know Maude is short? If not, why are we mentioning that she has to stand on her tippy-toes to look out the peephole? And do we really have to know that her nose is right up to the surface of the door? It seems obvious that this is how one looks through a peephole.

And of course she crosses the room one step at a time! How else would she get there? Look for places in your work where you can condense action. If the getting up isn't important, the scene could start with Maude looking out the peephole thinking that this better be important since it interrupted her favorite show and nightly glass of wine.

Don't layer in extra details just because you can. Layer in those kinds of details only if they're important. Otherwise you're giving readers information they think they'll need later on, when it's really just minutiae. You're loading them down with unnecessary words.

Word Repetition

All writers have at least one or two errors they catch themselves doing time and again. One of my own consistent blunders is word repetition. Sometimes I feel like I only know a hundred words and I keep reusing them over and over. Having a good vocabulary is essential for a writer, and for the most part, I feel up to par. So why do I often have the same word crop up three or four times in one page? I don't know. It's almost like a little hiccup on my part. I'll use the word "report" as a noun in one sentence and as a verb in the next and not notice until I reread that section later with a critical eye.

In talking to other writers, this is a fairly common faux pas, so if you find yourself guilty of this, don't be too hard on yourself. It's easy to fix once you're aware of it, and with time, it seems to happen less. Just be on the lookout.

Also something to watch for—starting each sentence or paragraph in a similar way.

He thought . . . He looked . . . He stood . . . If you notice this kind of thing in your writing you'll know it's time to mix things up.

Clarity

I once attended a critique group where a writer wrote two pages of back-and-forth conversation without dialogue tags. Just line after line of talking, with nothing indicating which characters were saying the words. When someone in the group mentioned he had difficulty following who was saying what, the writer said, "I did that on purpose. I want the reader to *wonder* who is speaking." His voice was so smug that we all let the matter drop (some people don't want to be helped), but speaking personally I can tell you that his stylistic choice didn't pique my curiosity. Instead I found it annoying. If I came across that scene in a novel, I would have stopped reading and abandoned the book.

Don't make readers work too hard. Yes, you know who is speaking. Let them in on the fun.

By the same token, ground your readers. If the characters are in a coffee shop or driving in a car, make this known right from the start of the scene. Don't make your readers figure out what should be obvious. It will not serve the story well, and you'll risk losing them.

Dialogue

Dialogue can be so much fun to write that beginning writers tend to overdo it. Including everything every character says can slow down the pace, and trust me, you don't want to do that. A brisk pace is what keeps people reading.

Writer Amy Bloom says, "Dialogue is not conversation. It is conversation's greatest hits." Sometimes more can be conveyed with a smirk or a wink than in multiple lines of dialogue. Other times, condensing dialogue might be in a scene's best interest.

In other instances, summarizing dialogue can be a useful strategy. Here's an example:

While Maude made small talk about the weather and how few tomatoes her garden had yielded that summer, Bruno shifted in his chair. Would she never shut up? He looked at his watch, but Maude didn't get the hint. She rambled on, telling him what the doctor had said about her blood pressure and how expensive her prescriptions were now compared to last year. Finally, after twenty minutes that felt more like an hour, he stood up, interrupting her monologue. "I have to go," he said.

You can imagine that Maude's end of the conversation could easily take up a page if it had been written as dialogue, and really, who wants that? Not me, not you, and certainly not Bruno. It's not important that we know exactly what was said. All we need to know is that Maude was rambling and Bruno was impatient, and the paragraph above managed to convey that just fine.

Scenes with characters conversing while sitting drinking coffee can be dull, even if the dialogue is sparkling or insightful. This type of thing is known as "talking heads." Person A talks, then Person B talks, Person A adds cream and stirs, Person B takes a sip, and repeat. Yes, people are talking and there is some action, albeit slight, but it's dreadfully boring. Why not take a page from the TV show *Law & Order* and have the people doing something else while they're talking? (Haven't you always wondered why the guy keeps unloading the truck while Stabler and Benson are asking him about one of his employees?) Make the thing they're doing relevant to the story, either to illuminate what the discussion is about, make a point about the person's character, or to foreshadow some future event. Otherwise it will seem random.

Clichés and Alliteration

Like a bat out of hell. As black as coal. Take the leap. As gentle as a lamb. She made me jump through hoops. A postage stamp–sized lot. He had an axe to grind.

Clichés. We all use them as shorthand for getting an idea across, but in fiction, they're looked upon as lazy writing. Try to avoid them if possible.

Using clichés in dialogue is somewhat more acceptable, because people do talk that way. Still, if you can find a more interesting way to say something, give that a go instead.

Alliteration, sometimes defined as several similar sounds in succession, is another thing to avoid. It might be oh so tempting to write something clever like, "Bruno bellowed at the bossy busboy." Don't do it. The reader will get pulled out of the story, and suddenly your novel will just become words on a page. Words that start with *b*.

Again, you don't want to do anything that distracts the reader.

Pet Peeves

Pet peeves. Every writer has them. If you're in a writers' group, you probably already know which member will call you out for clichés and who absolutely hates the word *moist*. I once had a critique partner who hated when a character "exited" the room. The word *exit* really chafed at her for some reason.

My sister Kay is an excellent editor. One time, after going over one of my manuscripts, she asked me (with kindness, but some frustration), "Do you have *any* idea how semicolons work?" After that, I made a point to learn, although sadly, I still get it wrong sometimes.

As for me, I have a few pet peeves of my own. My emotional response to these things goes far beyond the degree of error. I really don't know what my problem is, but I hate it when people use the word *lightening* when they mean *lightning*. Lightning is the flash of light in the sky you see during a thunderstorm. Lightening is what happens when color fades. I get itchy when I see them used interchangeably.

I'm equally annoyed when people mix up the words *loose* and *lose*. Correct usage: "Keep the dog on the leash so he doesn't get *loose.* You wouldn't want to *lose* your dog, would you?" To me it doesn't seem that hard to keep these two words straight, but I often see them used incorrectly, so apparently some people find it confusing. Double check, if you're not sure.

Another pet peeve? I cringe when people write about an era like the 1960s and put an apostrophe between the zero and the *s.* He grew up during the 1960s. No apostrophe.

I know it's a small thing, but it bugs me. Probably almost as much as my semicolon use bothered Kay. We all have something.

CHAPTER 9

Storytelling

Storytelling is the heart of the novel, the thing most people think about when they consider writing a book. What happens in your story, and to whom does it happen? And will anyone care about the characters currently residing in your head, trying to get out? And why do you have so much trouble getting the words down when it's all so clear in your mind? Believe me, I know the feeling of wanting to write a novel but being held back for some inexplicable reason.

There are some good reasons for putting it off until later. I believe writing fiction requires uninterrupted time, some physical room, and maybe most importantly—emotional space. The first two are self-explanatory, I think, but defining emotional space is a little trickier. If you're going through a period in your life where you're caring for a baby or small children, or helping a family member or friend going through an emotional, mental, or physical problem, you may not be able to write. If you're the one going through a major crisis, that goes double.

Writing a novel requires immersing yourself in a fictional world and experiencing the actions and emotions along with the characters. If the real world is sucking up everything you've got, you might not have any more to give.

I've been there, and it's frustrating. Agents think they're busy? Try spending twenty-four hours with the mother of a teething infant or the spouse of someone with dementia, and then we'll talk about busy. If this is you, if you're currently dealing with something so big you feel like it might swallow you up, you have my sympathies. I am so sorry that you're going through this. I'm not a hugger by nature, but honestly, if I were nearby, I'd give you a hug. I hope you get a reprieve from your situation and soon. A good night's sleep would be a start, I know. Everything seems hopeless when you're exhausted.

Try to take care of yourself, if at all possible. You've been given a herculean task, so cut yourself a break. If and when you do write your novel, it probably won't be about teething babies or caring for the elderly or going through chemo, but you'll still be able to use the myriad of emotions you've experienced during this time. And the stories running through your head will still be there when you're ready to type the words. Take it from someone who put off writing a novel for more than two decades—it's never too late.

Once you have the emotional space, some periods of uninterrupted time, and a place to work, writing a novel is very doable. This is not finding a cure for cancer or inventing a time machine (although if you're capable of doing one of those things, definitely work on that instead). This is putting words on a page. All kinds of people have done it, ranging from the most brilliant minds to those who are not so swift. I have no doubt you can do it too. Will you? That's entirely up to you. No one will sit at your elbow encouraging you as you go, I can tell you that much. It can be a lengthy, solitary process, made easier if you enjoy your own company.

Will you write a great novel right away? Maybe. It happens. It's also likely that your first novel won't be great. Still, you'll have done it, which is more than most people can say. And if you do it once, you can do it again.

The Who, What, and How of Your Novel (Or, What to Decide Before You Begin)

I can't tell you how you should begin writing your novel, but I can tell you how it works for me.

Before I even start, there are a few decisions to be made. As I said earlier, I'm not someone who plots out my books ahead of time. Instead, I'm what is known as a "pantser," someone who "flies by the seat of their pants." I don't feel like this label quite accurately fits me, though, because the pantser moniker implies pulling something out of thin air, creating story elements on the spot, which frankly sounds terrifying to me. In my regular life, I'm a planner. I don't like surprises; I leave the house early to allow time for traffic jams and train crossings. I'm certainly not the kind of free spirit who would sit down at my keyboard and expect a novel to pour out of my fingertips. I do plan, just not to the extent that a plotter does.

Before I write word one, I settle on a few things. Whose story is this?

Readers like to experience stories through the characters. An experienced novelist can have a huge cast of characters and flip between them, tying all of the many, many story threads up at the very end. I am not experienced enough to pull off this kind of thing, and most likely you aren't either. Focus on one primary character, maybe two. You will have more characters than this, of course, but the story will be told through the main character(s). Deciding upfront who gets the lead makes things much easier.

The next decision—what kind of novel is this? And what age group is it geared toward? I no longer worry about having a great marketing hook or fitting into a specific category or genre, but I like to have a sense of what the book will encompass. As my authorial voice has evolved, some common elements have emerged in all of my books. Will my new novel have elements of magical realism or aspects of the paranormal with some humorous overtones? Yes, please! And a happy ending? Of course!

Now I just have to decide how much magical realism and humor is appropriate for this particular novel. And do I want the ending to be gloriously happy or just filled with hope for a better tomorrow?

When the story reflects who I am as a writer, it just feels right. I know if the story gets too dark or some curse words slip in that I need to readjust it, because that's not me. This was something I realized as I went along in my writing journey. One book in particular made the point clear to me. My novel *The Long Way Home* details the experience of four women, strangers at the start, who wind up going on a cross-country road trip. Partway into the story, two of the women meet up with a bad guy who has a foul mouth. When something dramatic happens, he lets loose the F-bomb along with some other profanity.

It was the first time I'd used that particular word in one of my books. It didn't escape me that some people are very offended by what Ralphie in the movie *A Christmas Story* referred to as "the queen mother of dirty words." But for my character, in that situation, it fit. And really, it was only one word out of more than eighty-five thousand words. Would anyone even notice or care?

I finished the manuscript and turned it in. The book was approved by my acquiring editor, Terry Goodman, edited by a developmental editor, checked by a copyeditor, and then reviewed by a proofreader. It was headed into production when I had a change of heart and asked if I could reword the paragraph. Terry sighed, as he often did when I made his life more complicated, but sweetheart that he is, he made it happen. The file was emailed back to me, and I revised the sentences substituting milder expletives. Later, after the book came out, a blog reviewer said she liked my novels because she could recommend them both to her twelve-year-old daughter and her senior citizen mother. She went on to say that so many books today were loaded with unnecessary profanity and graphic scenes of violence and sex, and she was glad this wasn't the case with my books. Reading her take on my work validated my decision.

Now in saying this, I have to clarify that I have no objections to profanity or graphic scenes in other people's books. And if you've ever been at my house when I turned on the garbage disposal not realizing a spoon had dropped in, you'll know I'm capable of letting a few swear words rip. But for my books, it goes against my writing style. To me, finding a writing voice is like wearing clothes that fit. If you ever see me in a turtleneck, you'll know something is really wrong. I can't stand stretchy fabric up against my neck. Turtlenecks are great for other people, but not for me. Same thing for swear words. Ideal for some novels, just not mine. When you find the writing voice and style that works for you, you'll know. Hand in glove.

Once I've established the *who* and *what* of the novel, it's time to come up with *how* I'm going to tell the book. I start with selecting the point of view (POV). My novels are written in either first person or third person, and that's my preference as a reader, so that's what I'll cover here.

Before I begin to write, I need to know how this book is going to be presented to the reader. Will it be told in first person, and if so, will it be told just by one character or more than one? First person is sometimes preferred by beginning writers because it seems easier. After all, the character is telling the story, in the same way we would verbalize a story in real life. *Easily Amused* is told entirely in Lola's first person point of view, starting with the following sentence: "When I saw a group of my neighbors clustered on the sidewalk in front of Mrs. Cho's house, I was sure they were talking about me."

Pretty simple, right? We see the scene through the main character, the "I" who we come to learn is Lola Watson, a woman as lonely as she is antisocial. Someone who wants her life to be different, even as she refuses to make any changes.

Young adult novels are often told in first person, which creates immediacy if done well. Some of the old private eye novels did this most effectively. Raymond Chandler comes to mind as an author who did an expert first person point of view.

First person can be big fun to write, but it comes with a limitation. The reader only knows what the POV character knows.

It is possible to have different characters tell the story in first person point of view shifts in different chapters, but that's a tricky proposition. Their voices should be distinct, and there should be a specific reason why that particular character is chosen to tell that part of the story. I wrote a young adult series called *Edgewood*, in which the four main characters witness an astronomical event and discover they have superpowers. The first book in the series is told entirely in the POV of the main character, Russ Becker, but by the time I wrote the second book in the series, *Wanderlust*, I felt it was necessary to have some of the chapters told from another first person POV, by a girl named Nadia, who is also Russ's love interest. I gave the choice a lot of thought. Ultimately it came down to how best to tell the story. Some things are decided by instinct, and this was one of them.

The other most common POV choice, third person, can allow more range, while giving the reader the impression that there hasn't been a switch at all. In *A Scattered Life,* the POV switches between the three women, with each chapter belonging entirely to one of the three. So in a chapter by Audrey, the mother-in-law, the reader is only privy to Audrey's interior monologue, her thoughts and feelings, as the scene plays out. Even if all three of the characters are in the scene, the POV in that chapter never wavers from the chosen character. This is an excerpt of a scene from Audrey's point of view:

> She'd use Walt's car. It was a dark blue, midsized sedan, less likely to be noticed than her white station wagon. Walt wouldn't think anything of it. Audrey often used his car when hers was low on gas or if she was going somewhere where parallel parking might be involved. Over the weekend she decided Monday Night Football would be the perfect time to slip out. With enough cold beers in the

fridge and the chips and dip already set up, Jeffrey and Walt might not even notice she'd left.

Monday afternoon she moved Walt's car onto the street, and she slipped her field binoculars under the front seat. It was unlikely Walt would move it before Thomas left. Since Walt retired, he was a creature of precise habit. If he hadn't left the house by noon, he was home for the day. With the Packers facing the Minnesota Vikings later that evening, it was doubtful he'd even leave his recliner.

It is possible to use a combination of third and first POV in the same book. I did it but not until I had more than ten books behind me. In *From a Distant Star* most of the book is told from Emma's first person POV. A few chapters, however, are sprinkled in as third person accounts. This includes the opening chapter, which is told from the point of view of Mack, the dog. Most people were fine with that choice, including me (and since it was my book I considered it a win).

Once you've established your preferred POV, you might want to think about structure. Or not. Don't freak out if you don't have any definite ideas about how your book should be shaped. It's entirely possible the structure may come together organically as you piece the chapters together. Sometimes the author decides to structure a novel in a nontraditional way. I've read books where the story is bookended by the character as a much older person, telling about an earlier time in his or her life. Sara Gruen's novel *Like Water for Elephants* uses this method with great success.

I'd always thought it would be fun to write a book with alternating third person chapters, when the characters don't know each other, but their paths intersect. I got my chance when I wrote a novel called *Hello Love.* The story revolves around an adorable little dog named Anni who belongs to Dan, a widower with a teenage daughter. Anni is lost when she's stolen from Dan's front yard by a carful of rowdy drunks. Andrea, recently divorced, saves Anni from the dog snatchers and decides to keep her.

Dan and Andrea's story is played out in alternating chapters. Dan's chapter, then Andrea's chapter, and back to Dan, and so on. They cross paths multiple times, and it turns out they know some of the same people, but they don't make the Anni connection until the end. For this book I was very much influenced by old movies, the delightful kind that make you groan with all the obvious coincidences. One person gets off an elevator, just missing the other who is getting into the adjacent elevator, that kind of thing. Each time I wrote a Dan chapter, I'd be nervously thinking, *I wonder what's happening with Andrea right now.* Luckily, by the time I was done with Dan's section, an idea for the next part, Andrea's chapter, would pop into my head. I had a lot of fun writing it, and the dog on the cover was a big selling point.

If you have no idea how you want to structure your novel, don't worry about it. A novel in the process of being written is a fluid thing. Just write. You can add things later, move scenes around, take things out. Don't sweat it. You're not carving this into a block of wood. Nothing's permanent until you say it's permanent. Have fun with it.

Easier said than done, you say? Read on, kind reader.

The Plot Thickens

You know who your main character is, you've selected a point of view, and you have an idea of the type of novel you'd like to write. Now what?

You don't know? If the thought of making a mistake is paralyzing to you, I've got something that might help, and here it is:

no one cares. This is sad but true. If you're working on your first novel, no one yet knows you're writing a tome that once completed will put all other novels to shame. You're writing in secret, so you're free to do as you wish. Type all the F-bombs you want. Or not. Your call. Have your characters do something wild and crazy that no one in their right mind would do. Write pages of conversation with no dialogue tags just because. Who's going to stop you? No one, that's who! At some point your book will have to make sense for readers, but right now it's all yours. You can mess it up if you want to.

Now that we have that out of the way, shake your hands like people do in movies before playing the piano and begin. Ready, set, go!

You still got nothing?

I sympathize, and I also have a suggestion: don't do what I did. My first few novels were written by instinct. I had no idea what I was doing, and I was well aware of that fact. Other writers gave me feedback, literary agents gave suggestions (some that helped, some that just muddied the waters), and I voraciously read novels with an eye toward cracking the code. I stumbled through the process and made it out the other side, but it wasn't the easiest or best way. I want better for you.

At some point in my writing journey, I decided to check out a few screenplays, thinking they might give me different insights into the storytelling process. Screenplays are about ninety pages, about a third to a fourth of the length of one of my novels. They're the stripped-down version of a story, consisting of dialogue and action with a tiny amount of stage direction. What a screenplay lacks is the interior parts—the characters' musings, as well as the description and scene setting you see in novels. The best part? You can find screenplays online for free. I read a few and found them fascinating, but I still had trouble applying the structure to my own storytelling.

I did a little more Googling and came across a book: *The Writer's Journey: Mythic Structures for Writers* by Christopher Vogler. I'd read dozens of books on writing by this point, but *The Writer's Journey* was in a whole different league. It spoke to me. I felt like Christopher Vogler had given me a storytelling map. I read the book and reread it, and then I took a step back and watched a PBS series called *Joseph Campbell: The Power of Myth*. Joseph Campbell was a mythologist and scholar who discovered universal narrative patterns in storytelling throughout the ages. Christopher Vogler adapted Campbell's work for his job as a story analyst for the movie industry.

Human beings have told stories as long as they've been able to communicate, and Vogler's book asserts that "all stories consist of a few common structural elements found universally in myths, fairy tales, dreams, and movies." He breaks down what he calls "The Hero's Journey" into twelve parts and then goes on to explain and illustrate what each step means. He also details various character archetypes. What I love most is the way he correlates the varying aspects to popular movies. Illustrating the elements this way made it crystal clear to me.

I found, in a bit of reverse engineering, that the novels I'd already written had loosely followed the pattern described in *The Writer's Journey*. What Campbell had suggested as being true for most members of the human race was true for me. Without even realizing it, I had somehow internalized how to write a story and pulled this knowledge out when I wrote my books. If it's true for me, it's true for you too. All of us have read books, seen movies, heard jokes, overheard strangers talking in doctors' waiting rooms. We know how to tell a story.

Keep that in mind when you're writing, and learn to trust the process.

Every time I write a novel, I wind up flipping through *The Writer's Journey*. I don't use it as a paint-by-numbers writing manual. Instead, I find it helpful in jump-starting my creativity when I get stuck, or gauging how I'm doing as I go along. Sometimes I don't open it until I'm nearly done with a novel, and I'm always amazed at how I've unwittingly incorporated story elements from "The Hero's Journey" into my own book. Not every story needs to have every element, and they don't necessarily have to be in order. The book is a guide, a help for those times when you might want to shine a light on a problem. Writing a novel can be a very solitary venture, and it doesn't hurt to get some outside guidance.

Another good book for writers interested in breaking down the elements of a plot is *Save the Cat* by Blake Snyder. Although this book is intended for screenplay writers, much of the information can apply to novels as well. For me, personally, it wasn't as helpful as Vogler's book, but I've heard other writers swear by *Save the Cat*, particularly for the "Blake Snyder Beat Sheet," which is made up of fifteen essential "beats" or plot points that all stories should contain.

I can recommend both books and Campbell's work for anyone interested in finding out more about classic storytelling. If you don't want to purchase the books, much of the information is available online. And if after reading these books you still don't know how to start your novel, you can always rely on the old standby: a stranger comes to town.

Now that I've covered the overarching shape of plot, I'll give you a few thoughts on the writing within.

Reader, Meet Story

Imagine you're invited to a cocktail party where you don't know anyone except the person holding the affair. Right after you arrive, the host ushers you over to a group of eight people and immediately goes around the circle giving each person's name and what he or she does for a living. You try to take it all in, but panic under the pressure of trying to keep all this information straight. Ultimately it gets to be too much, and you're lucky if you remember two or three names. By this time, you're stressed out and want to go home.

Don't do this to your readers. When your novel opens, welcome readers in, take their coats, and let them get settled. Introduce them to one, maybe two characters and set the hook before you ambush them with too many people and too much detail. It's tempting to introduce everyone at once. Don't do it. It's a novel; there will be more pages later on.

About That Hook

The whole idea is to hold the reader's attention. There's no hard-and-fast rule in this area, but I've found that a bit of intrigue helps. As writers we always think that we need something complicated and intricate to hook the reader, but really all you need to do is plant a seed. Starting a book with the line, "It was the third-worst day of my life," will make the reader wonder why it was a terrible day and what happened on the other two, even worse days. It won't keep a reader's interest for three hundred pages, of course, but presumably there will be other plot points later on to pull the reader along.

A situation can pose a question as well. If a character arrives late to a family gathering with her hair mussed and clothing covered in blood, and doesn't want to talk about it, there's your seed. What exactly is going on? As a reader, I'd be curious.

Putting a question out there works as well. Say there's a surprise party and the person organizing it is convinced Grandma will love having fifty people yell, "Surprise!" when she comes home from the opera, while another character predicts she'll be furious when she sees her estranged daughter there. Most readers will stick around to see how it plays out.

And lastly, end each chapter with something that leaves the reader wanting more. A package arrives and we don't know what's in it. Or maybe there's a knock on the door. Who could it be at this time of night? Or maybe a character leaves and promises he'll be right back, but the situation is worrisome and the other character, the one left behind, has a bad feeling that she'll never see him again. You get the idea. So many terrific authors do this to great effect. The book that immediately comes to mind is Dan Brown's *The Da Vinci Code*.

You might find ending your chapters with such an obvious hook is an affront to your literary sensibilities. If so, adjust accordingly. It can be done in a much more subtle way. No matter what your writing style or genre, your book can benefit from layering in some kind of intrigue. As novelists, we fail if the reader sets the book down and never finishes it. Make it hard for the reader to stop reading.

Climb into the Character

Readers like to live vicariously through fiction. As a novelist, you are going to wear the character like a suit and relate things from his point of view so the reader can experience the story through that character.

Something to keep in mind: you're seeing the world through your character's eyes, not watching it like a movie. Say your character drives back to the old neighborhood where he grew up, after having been gone for thirty years. This is not the place to drop in a description right out of *Wikipedia*. You don't need to mention when the houses were built or that it was a working-class neighborhood. No one needs to know the approximate square footage of each house. Those kinds of things come off as info dumps, something you should avoid at all costs.

What you can do is have the character think about how the houses used to seem bigger when he was a kid, and how he remembers when the neighborhood dads would come home from the factory at the end of their shift and how the sight of their cars pulling into the driveways meant it was time to go inside and wash up for dinner. Maybe his old house is run-down now and the lawn appears scrubby and overgrown with weeds, and this pains the man because he remembers how his father took such pride in keeping everything nice. Your character sees the neighborhood from his vantage point, so that's how you need to relate it.

Beginning novelists usually do a good job with two of the senses: sight and sound. They remember to include the visual descriptions and the audio (dialogue and an occasional random noise), but that's about it. Don't forget to include at least one other sense in every scene. It doesn't need to be described in detail. Even mentioning your character taking a sip of cold lemonade will suffice. It's not necessary to describe the pulp or lack thereof, or go into detail about the degree of sourness. Readers will mentally insert their own lemonade-drinking experience into the mix.

Touch is a great one that's not always utilized as much as it could be. Pulling a sweater over your head might feel scratchy or make your hair staticky. (Man, I hate that.) And don't forget that a tactile experience, like any other sensory experience, can be linked to an emotion. In bed, the weight of a heavy quilt might be comforting or it might feel confining.

I have a terrible sense of smell, so I tend not to use it very much in my books, but I love reading it in other people's novels. To me, most things smell bad or good and I have trouble determining much more than that. I went to a routine doctor's appointment once, and he apologized for the smell of the floor wax. I assured him it was fine, that I couldn't smell it. "Not at all?" he said, alarmed. I wound up getting an MRI to make sure I didn't have a brain tumor. I'm happy to say the MRI didn't reveal any problems. They've never been able to determine why my smeller is deficient, but there are times I've been told I should consider myself lucky.

Backstory

When I talk about backstory, I'm not referencing the use of two storylines in a novel, one that runs earlier in time and one set in contemporary time. Sometimes you see this in books—the present-day story is, for instance, a detective trying to solve a decades-old crime. The other story, the one set in the past, leads up to the crime and is revealed in pieces as the detective unearths more information. Yes, the past story is technically backstory, but in this instance, it's absolutely necessary and an integral part of the plot.

The backstory I'm cautioning you against overusing is the type that explains everything leading up to the current story. I've done this sort of thing myself, and at the time, I felt the backstory was absolutely essential. It was not.

I understand that it's tempting, if, say, a couple in your story is divorced, to think you have to do a lot of explainy-explainy about *why* they wound up getting divorced, but chances are a few lines will fill in the blanks quite nicely. If you don't believe me, try it both ways. Write the more detailed version of the divorce and then do a shorter passage, summing it up as briefly as possible. When you're finished, read both versions. I think you'll find that sometimes less is more.

In cases where backstory is needed, see if you can weave it into the text in small doses along the way. Revealing bits of information as the story progresses can be used to answer the questions placed earlier in the book, which feels like payoff to the reader.

Think about what purpose the backstory fulfills. Is it really necessary? And if so, is there a way to condense it without reducing its effectiveness? Consider minimizing backstory as a challenge to be met.

Contradictions

When you're rereading your pages, make sure the actions of the characters, no matter how small, are actually plausible. If, for instance, a character has a pronounced limp, he most likely would not be able to outrun the bad guys.

Think about reactions as well. If someone has just found out her parents have been murdered, she'll probably be reeling from disbelief and grief first, before she vows, fist to sky, to find the killers.

Even the smallest actions need to be checked. In the sentence, "She took a sip of wine while shrugging off her jacket," the action would be nearly impossible, since pulling a sleeve over a wine glass would be quite a feat. In the writer's mind, it might be obvious that she took a sip of wine *and then* shrugged off her jacket, but that's not what the words said. Just a slight reworking would make it clear.

Your job as the writer is to provide a seamless reading experience. Readers want to settle in and immerse themselves in a good story. Don't make them work to figure out what you meant.

My BFF, Scrooge

At one time, writers were cautioned against creating unlikeable main characters. The consensus was that readers didn't want to spend time with characters they wouldn't be friends with in real life. This always puzzled me. What about Scarlett O'Hara, Ebenezer Scrooge, and Dexter? Fascinating characters all, but no one you'd want to be friends with. More recently, there's Amy in *Gone Girl*. Who'd want to hang out with her?

The whole likeability thing was doubly confusing because when I made a concerted effort to make my characters likeable, the feedback I got was that they were dull. Vanilla. Uninteresting. Boring. What's a writer to do? 'Twas a puzzlement.

Thankfully, I'm hearing less talk about characters being likeable as of late. It seems that as long as the reader is along for the journey, a character can embody all sorts of personality traits. Still, there are some things to keep in mind.

I can speak to this personally as I've gotten flak over a few of the characters in my novels. In my experience, it's best to avoid having a character who is too needy or too snarky. One person's devoted love is another person's unbearable clinginess. Your version of clever sarcasm could be interpreted as arrogant and insufferable.

Any character who is unkind to friends is a big old douchebag, or so I've been told. A woman or girl who refers to another female as a slut, even if it's just a thought, sort of in jest, and is not actually said aloud, will be branded a terrible, awful human being by your readers. As will you, by association. This will incur wrath like you wouldn't believe. It's probably best to just take that word out of your vocabulary, both in writing and life. There's no good reason to use it.

Make sure your character has friends. One is fine, two is better. If the friends aren't important to the story, they can be casually referenced. If friends aren't mentioned, readers will assume he or she has no friends, which can influence their feelings toward the character and not in a good way. In a novel, friends can be helpful in giving the main character advice (good and bad), and they can be a source of information the main character might not be privy to otherwise ("I wasn't supposed to tell you this, but...").

What do readers like in a fictional character?

I've found that readers connect with a character in pain. It helps the audience to care about that character and what happens to him. I think this empathy is part of who we are as human beings. It can be a physical, mental, or emotional pain, but it has to be valid. The situation has to ring true to the reader. The character in pain can't be whiny or dwell on it. There's nobility in suffering without complaint. The qualities we admire in real life also apply in fiction.

Readers also love characters who are kind to animals and small children. You'll score points if you show someone rescuing an animal, especially if she does it at risk to herself. Of course, don't do it randomly. Something as significant as rescuing an animal has to exist in a book for a reason or it will frustrate readers. They'll get to the end of the book, think back, and wonder, *What was the point of that?*

Try to remember that the main character should be the hero of his own story. So if, for instance, you're writing a young adult novel and your fifteen-year-old main character needs to get somewhere in the middle of the night, it's not a good idea for him to wake his parents to ask for a ride. Trust me, he'll figure out something on his own, and it will be far more interesting than having his dad drive him. Readers admire heroes who are self-sufficient.

Another great trait? Self-sacrifice. Putting others ahead of themselves. Who doesn't love that? Readers like characters who take action because they know it's the right thing to do. We all like to imagine that if we were in a dangerous situation, we'd do something heroic. Fiction is a way to vicariously live out that dream.

Time Traveler

You say you've always wanted to travel through time and space? Congratulations, as an author you can and should do both. When you write a novel, you are the master of your own fictional world, able to fast-forward or rewind, traversing great distances effortlessly. Go ahead, jump over the boring parts and take your reader right to the good stuff.

Back when I talked about contradictions, this was an example I listed: If someone just found out her parents had been murdered, she'd probably be reeling from disbelief and grief first, before she vows, fist to sky, to find the killers. Say that this was an actual scene in your novel. If your first draft omitted the character's natural reaction, the disbelief and grief, the story might not ring true for the reader. How much better would it be to show how the character takes the news, then cut to three months later, where she vows, at that point, to find the killer? The three months don't have to be shown. Just end one chapter with the character getting the news, and start the next chapter three months later. If you want to summarize what happens during the three months, go ahead and fill us in, but make it brief.

Voilà! Time travel. Not as exciting as a ride in the Tardis, but cool nonetheless.

If the concept doesn't come naturally to you, look to movies and television. Transitions happen so easily on the screen. One minute a group of characters is given the secret treasure map; the next minute we cut to them getting off the plane in South America. No one says, "When did they book the flight? Why didn't we see them packing?" We don't care about the in-between stuff; we just want the story to move forward. Ta-da!

If this whole treasure map/South America scenario were a scene in a book, the author could use the jump forward as a way to leverage the intrigue I mentioned earlier. Say one of the characters, we'll call him Ryan, doesn't want to go to South America with the others. In fact, he outright refuses to go, saying, "Never gonna happen. Over my dead body!" The next chapter has the group exiting the plane, Ryan straggling last, dragging his carry-on behind him. The reader will keep reading, wondering how Ryan's friends managed to convince him to go. The author can then relate, either in dialogue or in a character's memory, what actually happened. (If I were writing that scene, I'd make it so he lost a bet. A very complicated, far-fetched bet.) If this series of events had been written in sequential order (first Ryan refusing to go, then the bet, then him losing the bet, then the group going to South America, etc.) the pacing would have been slower, and it would have lacked the element of intrigue. Doing it with the skip allows the story to move forward and backward in one scene, while piquing the reader's interest at the same time.

A character's memories can be a method of time travel in fiction. A chapter can take place in the story's present time, but jump back through the years via our character's memory. Just be sure this type of thing serves a purpose, or your novel will get bogged down with the dreaded backstory.

Sometimes writers get hung up on transitions, the introductory sentences that explain the change in time and place. I once spent an hour playing with the wording that would convey a story had jumped ahead almost a month. After realizing I was making it more complicated than it needed to be, I settled on starting the chapter with, "Three weeks later . . ." When I was done with the book, I went over the text again and reworked it so it read a little more gracefully, but even if I hadn't, "Three weeks later," was a serviceable transition. It doesn't have to be fancy. It just has to get the job done.

Timeline

Maybe this won't be a problem for you, but it has been for me, so I thought I'd mention it. Because I'm the master of all I survey in my fictional worlds, I play pretty fast and loose with time, and sometimes I get tangled up in it. I've had early readers point out that if months have elapsed over the course of the book, then the season would have changed, or they inform me that three days after Tuesday would make it Friday, not Sunday. Oops.

For one of my books I finally mapped out the sequence of events using a calendar. And then I had to go forward and backward to fit in the flashbacks and fast-forwards. Oh, good grief. What a pain. I've discovered that it's better to keep track as I go along. So that's what I do now.

Location, Location, Location

It's easier than ever to set a story wherever you want, even if it's a country or city you've never visited. There are firsthand accounts, video clips, and satellite images online. Most writers carefully research details about the weather, culture, and customs, but I'd like to issue another caution, one that sometimes gets overlooked.

Make sure the names are appropriate to the locale, or it will not ring true to people living there. I once read a book set in the community of Lake Geneva, Wisconsin, where the lake was referred to as "Lake Geneva." You'd think that would be correct, but in fact, the lake is called "Geneva Lake." I have no idea why it's switched around, and it didn't particularly bother me, but there were readers from the area who mentioned the goof in reviews.

This also applies to people's names. I've lived in Wisconsin my whole life (a fact that does not impress too many people), and I know Wisconsin names. Not all of them, of course, but I've gone to school, worked at different jobs, stood in line at the DMV, and so forth. There are some types of names prevalent in this part of the state.

I once critiqued a friend's novel manuscript. The story took place in southeastern Wisconsin, but the friend was a transplant, so she was, as they say, "not from around here." As I read her story, which I loved, I realized that the names bothered me. She'd picked some really cool surnames, none of which sounded like Wisconsin names.

Of course you're free to pick whatever names you want, and not all of them have to have strong ties to the area, but sprinkling in a few will make the story seem more accurate for the local folks.

Something to keep in mind.

Keeping the Pace

How do you speed things up and slow things down in your story? It's not as complicated as you'd think. The space on the page correlates with the pacing of the story. If you want to slow things down, take more time describing the action and the scene: the unseasonably warm weather, the crunch of his boots on the gravel, the look on her face when she realizes she's been betrayed.

If you want to speed things up, shorter sentences and paragraphs give the illusion the story is proceeding at a faster clip.

For dramatic moments, make sure the space on the page is commensurate with the weight of the action. I once read a scene in a novel where a character got stabbed, but I didn't realize it because the author described the stabbing as the flash of the blade, a forward thrust, and a woman crying out. The whole thing was covered in one sentence, so I assumed the man with the knife had just waved it in her direction to scare her. A few paragraphs later, when she was bleeding, I was like, *Wait a minute—did she get stabbed?*

I stopped and went back and reread that one sentence. *Huh. I guess she was stabbed.*

I can only speculate that the author wanted to keep the pace going, while still maintaining a literary voice. Perhaps he did not want to dumb it down for readers like me, but in my opinion, someone getting stabbed deserves a few more words of explanation. Plus, it's a great dramatic moment, the kind I love to write. Why wouldn't you embellish it a bit?

Pacing problems are definitely fixable after the fact, so you don't need to stress about them as you're writing, but it's something to consider once the manuscript is finished and you're ready to revise.

Rule of Three

The rule of three is one of my favorite things to talk about when discussing writing. The rule of three, sometimes known as the power of three, suggests that information organized around the number three is funnier or more satisfying or more memorable. The three pattern crops up in children's stories (*Goldilocks and the Three Bears, The Three Little Pigs, The Three Billy Goats Gruff*), jokes (a panda, a horse, and a monkey walk into a bar), and in the theater (three-act plays).

Once you're aware of it, you'll see the number three everywhere. In phrases like, "Life, Liberty, and the pursuit of Happiness." And in court, when people about to testify are asked to tell "the truth, the whole truth, and nothing but the truth." Really, is all that necessary? Just tell the truth! But of course, repeating it three times drives the point home, and there's something lyrical about the way it's phrased as well.

We divide time into past, present, and future. The number three comes up in religion, nursery rhymes, and advertising slogans. Real estate agents talk about "location, location, location." Stories have a beginning, middle, and end.

For some reason, the human brain responds to the number three, and as a writer you can use this to your advantage. If you want to give your character a few friends and are undecided about the number, take a note from *Harry Potter, Nancy Drew*, and *The Three Musketeers* and make it a trio.

Here's an example using the rule of three as a plot device: create an event that occurs three times in a novel, with the first two times seemingly occurring one way and the third time creating the twist. A woman is being stalked by someone who leaves threatening messages, vandalizes her car, and leaves dead animals on her doorstep. Twice she notices a man in a red car watching her, and she's convinced it's her stalker. The third time she sees him, he leaps out of the car to save her from being attacked by the actual stalker, someone she knows.

Savvy readers might see this coming, so make sure to layer in lots of convincing evidence that points to the man in the car.

Another way to use the rule of three is by mentioning an object or event of importance three times. If a little old lady character pulls out a gun and saves the day at the end of a story and the gun has never been mentioned before this, readers will feel like you played a trick on them. *How convenient!* they might say. The rule of three would recommend mentioning it twice before. The first time something comes up we notice it; the second time we make a note of it; the third time is the "aha."

Show, Don't Tell

Much has been written about this, so I'll just touch on it briefly. Sometimes beginning writers take the axiom "show, don't tell," so literally as to take it to the opposite extreme. Telling is not inherently evil or amateurish, as some might imply. There are times when telling is just what's needed to relay the story. The trick is to differentiate when the novel is best served by telling and when showing is more appropriate.

Scenes with important action or emotional heft are best related through showing. We want readers to experience it as if they were there. But showing, as important as it is, also takes up a lot of space on the page. And there are times when we don't want to slow down the pace. This is when telling is useful.

Key information can be slipped in through telling in order to present it in a more concise way. Maybe we want to show a character arriving late to an important meeting at work. Turns out his job is on the line and this is his one chance to defend himself. One problem—the meeting is early in the morning and he's running late. If for pacing's sake we don't want to spend pages showing him getting stopped at a train crossing, getting stuck on the expressway, and experiencing other kinds of delays, we can use telling as a device to summarize. The character—I'll call him Ron—can be dashing through the hallways at work, thinking about how he'd be on time if only he hadn't overslept and if only he hadn't experienced all the problems on the drive to work. His thinking about it is essentially telling the reader what happened.

Another alternative would be having the receptionist make a snarky comment about how his boss is waiting for him, and Ron shooting back that it wasn't his fault, that he was stopped by a train. In this case, the telling is done via dialogue.

Don't take the old "show, don't tell" to be an absolute. Decide which one to use based on how best to relate your story to the reader.

Combining Scenes

Writers sometimes think about scenes so logically and linearly that it doesn't occur to them that they can double up events, making the scene more interesting and increasing its effectiveness. In my book *Edgewood*, I wanted to show the relationship between Russ and his ten-year-old nephew, Frank, so I did it on a trip to the comic book store where they run into Russ's teacher Mr. Specter, who is working behind the counter as a favor to the owner. As Frank goes to pay for his comic books, he empties the contents of his pocket out on the counter, and Mr. Specter sees a small stone. He offers Frank twenty dollars for it, which Frank happily accepts. In another chapter, Russ realizes the significance of the stone and confronts his teacher at school, saying he wants it back. Mr. Specter agrees but says Russ needs to come to his house later that night to get it.

Did Frank need to be at the store? Well, yes, the way it was written. But Russ could just as easily have had the stone in his pocket if Frank had asked him to hold on to it. He could have had the heart-to-heart talk with his nephew at home, then headed to the comic book store on his own. I thought it was much more interesting, however, to combine the two events. The same technique gave me an opportunity for the two to visit a frozen custard shop, where they encounter Frank's bully, the one who'd been giving him a hard time about not having a dad.

Combining a character's family with his school or work life is equivalent to having a party and inviting your work friends, your Grandma, and your best friends from high school. When worlds collide, things get much more interesting.

CHAPTER 10

Making an Emotional Connection

You know how sometimes you read a novel and just feel kind of meh about it? Perhaps the plot was riveting, the writing gorgeous, and the descriptions so accurate you felt like you were *there.* The book was great, better than most, but you wouldn't recommend it to a friend, and you don't really know why. A few weeks later it's hard to remember much about the book. Even the name of the main character is forgotten.

Very often, when I come across a book like this, the place where it falls short is in the emotional element. Sometimes reviewers will say they weren't pulled in, or didn't care about the characters. That they felt detached from what was happening in the story.

Some authors manage to instinctively set up their work to create an emotional connection. If you ask them how they manage to create stories that make readers laugh and cry, they'll shrug and say something like, "If I'm feeling it, I'm fairly sure my readers will too." I don't think they're keeping the secret to themselves; it's just that the process is so automatic to them that they've never felt the need to break it down.

It's not hard to learn, though, and once you have the knack it will come about naturally as part of your writing process.

Climb into the Character

Remember when we were talking about storytelling and the need to climb into the characters and experience the story through them? This is true of sensory experiences, dialogue, and action scenes, and it's true of emotional experiences as well.

In a workshop I once attended, a member brought a story to be critiqued. The writing was top-notch, the kind that always makes me envious. In the story, a woman who is driving becomes lost and somehow winds up in the bad part of town. As she pauses at a stop sign, a gang of men come out from nowhere and begin throwing rocks. The writing was so fabulous, we felt like we were there: the men approaching menacingly, the thunk of the rocks against the car, the cracking of the windshield radiating outward like a spider's web. The woman grips the steering wheel tightly and curses. As the men surround her car, she floors the accelerator and they jump out of the way. She escapes.

Just one thing was missing. Another participant brought it up before I could even put my finger on it. "Was she afraid?" he asked.

"A group of men attacked her car," the writer said. "Of course she was afraid."

Yeah, none of us got that.

Most women in that circumstance would be afraid, of course, but some women might get angry; others might take it in stride. The human race is as varied in their emotional responses as they are in everything else.

Readers want the full experience. Sight, sound, smells, emotion—all of it. We can watch things happen in movies and on TV and oftentimes we'll be touched emotionally, but reading a novel in which you experience everything along with the character is a unique experience. Give your readers the full heart-pounding, palm-sweating experience, complete with the thought process that goes along with it. Show readers the thoughts running through her mind: *Dear God, help me! Am I doing to die here and never see my husband and baby again?* Or: *If those bastards think they're getting me out of this car, they've got another thing coming.*

Emotional elements can be added through thoughts, physical responses, and sensory experiences. Making sure the reader is aware of the character's emotional state is imperative if you want to make that connection.

Tension

So often writing teachers talk about the importance of maintaining tension in fiction. In theory it makes sense, but beginning writers, and I was once one of them, are often not sure *how* to infuse tension into their fiction. Tension in fiction is different than tension in real life. For instance, two people arguing on the page does not constitute tension (except between them). Two people arguing as they hike through the woods, while unbeknownst to them they're being trailed by a stranger—now that's tension.

Creating tension is part of the emotional connection. Once readers are on the edge of their seat wondering what will happen next, they're involved and there's no turning back. Tension comes in not knowing. Readers delight in the unexpected, stories that have twists and turns. They love having some inside information about a character that might not seem important at the time it's revealed, but plays out later in a big way. Think of Indiana Jones in *Raiders of the Lost Ark*: "Why did it have to be snakes?"

Send a character to do something hard—confront the mean boss or open the door to the locked room, the one her grandmother warned her never to enter. Then up the stakes and make things more complicated. The character catches the boss doing something illegal and becomes a witness, or the room turns out to contain evidence of some big family secret. Then what happens? One thing should lead to the next and the next. Throw in unexpected complications and keep yourself open. Your imagination is a wild and wonderful place. Don't hold back.

Oh, and one more thing. If you can take a chapter out and the story still works, you probably don't need that chapter.

Emotional Shift

I once read a book on writing screenplays (I'm sorry, I can't remember which one!) that said each scene should end on a different emotional note than the one present at the beginning. So, for instance, if the main character is depressed at the beginning of the chapter, something should happen in the chapter to cause an emotional shift so that at the end the main character feels differently.

After I read that I went to my bookcase and flipped open a few of my favorite novels. Sure enough, all of the novelists I admired had employed this technique, perhaps unwittingly. When I went over my own books, I found the same to be true as well. I don't make a point to do this, but knowing about the concept means this is one more thing to check when I've completed a manuscript. It gives me a chance to tweak the emotional shift if need be.

CHAPTER 11

A Finished Novel

So, you've gone and done it—completed a book. Whether it was by writing a page a day for a year, or by writing two thousand words each day, five days a week, and finishing in two or three months, it doesn't matter. You accomplished something many people talk about but never do. Bravo! Bask in the glory. You are a novelist.

Now what?

Well, if your manuscript is like mine, it still needs some work. You're going to want to have some trusted readers go over the pages with an eye toward making the book better. Finding these trusted readers is no small thing. So many times, people make suggestions based on how *they* would do it, the result of which would turn your story into a completely different book. I've had readers suggest changing the spelling of a character's name, adding a pet to the plot, and requesting what I thought was unnecessary background information. At this point in my writing career, I consider everything, but I tend to rely on my instincts since they have served me well in the past. Don't forget that it's your book. Ultimately, it's up to you.

Instead of giving your beta readers free rein, ask them ahead of time to flag problems of clarity, continuity, and pacing. Did the book end too abruptly? Were there timeline issues? And of course, you always want to know about typos and errors in grammar and punctuation.

The main concern should be fixing mistakes. The second concern is addressing other issues. Ask your beta readers these kinds of questions: Are the main character's actions consistent with their personality? Were you bored? Confused? If so, at what point in the story were you bored or confused?

If you have several beta readers and only one person has a problem with something, it might just be them. Check with the others and ask specifically if they felt the same way.

If readers are bored, that's your cue to cut or condense the parts that are lagging.

Another question to ask might be about their emotional responses. If they felt disconnected from the characters, you need to go back and layer in additional elements to address this.

Once you've made all of these changes, the manuscript still needs to be edited. If you have the money to hire a professional, that's ideal. I didn't initially, so I relied upon my sister and other writers I'd connected with.

And then, the big question—to self-publish or to query agents and editors? That is entirely up to you. There are pros and cons to both.

I think you can guess I'm a huge fan of self-publishing. I'm biased, of course, because it worked out for me in a big way. My self-published books were the foot in the door to Amazon Publishing, and my wonderful partnership with them has led to other opportunities: audio books with Brilliance Audio, paperbacks with Houghton Mifflin Harcourt, and translation rights for my books being translated into five languages.

But you know what? I still self-publish some of my books. My young adult series, *Edgewood*, is self-published and so is a spooky, fun book called *Grimm House*, which I wrote for the middle-grade crowd. I made the choice to release the *Edgewood* series on my own, going purely on gut instinct. I had big plans for these books. I saw them appealing to all ages, coming out in audio, translated into other languages. I imagined them as graphic novels and movies. I sensed that my over-the-top enthusiasm was not matched by my publisher, so I opted to publish them myself. I incurred the expense of the editor and cover designer, but it was worth it to have the books match my vision for them. Right now, the first three are available in audio and have been translated into German, and I'm working on the fourth book in the series. I loved being able to release the books on my terms and on my timetable, which was also the case with *Grimm House.* It's worked out well for me.

I would love to work with Amazon Publishing on future books, but knowing I can always self-publish is something I'm glad to have in my back pocket. Before 2009, that wasn't the case.

I have friends who love their agents, who say they wouldn't want to do this without them. Every now and then I think I might be missing out. I wonder if my resistance to having someone take over the business details is depriving me of other opportunities, so twice more I wound up giving an agent a chance.

Agent Five emailed me sometime after the *Wall Street Journal* article ran. Several agents had contacted me, and as I said before, I politely declined, but this woman was persistent. She wanted to talk to me, just a talk, she said, to see if it made sense for me to have an agent to handle future transactions. I still wasn't sure I wanted an agent, but I admired her tenacity and said, if anything, I could use someone to shop television and movie rights. She was agreeable, mentioning that her agency had done some big deals in that area, so we arranged to meet when I would be in New York for the BookExpo America.

We met at a restaurant one Sunday morning. After exchanging pleasantries, I tried to steer the conversation to the reason I'd thought we'd met: to discuss her handling the sale of the television and movie rights of my books. She had other ideas. None of my books would be appropriate for those markets, she said, and then added that I needed to send her a copy of the contract for the movie option for *A Scattered Life*. She also added that she checked and her agency wouldn't allow her to represent a client for only television and movie rights. It just wasn't done.

I circled back to our original topic. None of the books would be suitable for film or television? How about Lifetime or Hallmark? No, she said, shaking her head, then explained that one of the two I mentioned was only doing stories about women in peril and the other was an almost impossible market to penetrate.

As we talked about my books, it was clear she didn't like them. I picked up on this based on her tone and the fact that she called my writing style "truncated." At one point, I said I hated doing paperwork and she said, "Me too!" I guess she didn't realize I was interviewing her for a job which would require her to do paperwork. It was like your tax guy telling you numbers and math aren't really his thing.

From there Agent Five took over the conversation. What I needed to do, she said, was sign with her, and she'd shop around my next women's fiction. I could fly out to New York and meet with editors, to get a feeling for who I'd like to work with. She said she might be able to get me a big advance, no promises, but it could be six figures.

I kept trying to tell her that I had a publisher I was extremely happy with and that I was already doing well with sales. Amazon Publishing had the first look at my next book. It was in my contract. To do what she was suggesting, I'd have to cut ties with them on the chance that I could publish elsewhere. It would be like quitting the best job you've ever had on the promise of *maybe* getting something better. I wasn't convinced there was something better out there. As I tried to explain, she waved away my words and kept talking about these other publishing houses. At one point, she said, "I don't understand why you don't want a *real* publisher."

By the end of the meeting, I knew our interests weren't aligned.

I continued on for the next few years, happily writing books and seeing them published until one summer when I wrote a children's book I called *Grimm House*. I loved the idea of getting the book into the hands of as many children as possible and knew that there were publishers who had specific inroads with schools and libraries. I also knew, through an acquaintance, an agent who had a terrific reputation in that area. I spoke with Agent Six, and after she read the book, she was enthused about possibly working with me.

Based on her suggestions, I did one round of revisions and sent the manuscript back. When Agent Six said she had more notes, I assumed it would be one last pass for typos and other small corrections. But, no. Agent Six had even more revision notes, requiring a complete rewrite of the book. I read over the notes, trying to think how I could redo the whole book and satisfy both of us, and came up with nothing. Agent Six wanted the magic in the book explained, suggested I add a plot thread that would make a pivotal chapter not work anymore, and also wanted me to add other elements. She also didn't think there was a clear enough character arc. There was so much, it made my heart sink. It wasn't that I didn't want to do the work. I just disagreed.

To my mind, all the things she mentioned had already been addressed or weren't necessary. I hated the idea of making random changes. I believe a book has a certain shape that can be destroyed by adding things in, taking them out, stretching it like taffy. And once that happens, there's the very real possibility of throwing off the pacing and affecting the tension. I grappled with what to do. What if Agent Six's ideas would take the book from good to great? She was smart and sincere. To her mind, the book really needed these changes. Was I just being stubborn? I went to bed one night miserable and woke up the next day with one immediate thought, coming in like a radio signal: *You don't have to do this.*

I decided to get it copyedited and then self-publish it. Good or bad, in the end it would be my book, and I'd be happy to take the credit or blame.

Agent Six had been so lovely that I regretted having to tell her that we weren't a good match. She was great about it, actually. Very gracious. I sent her an Open Table gift certificate. I'm sure it didn't fully compensate her for her time, but it made me feel better.

So, yeah. Me and agents are probably not going to happen. I've been an outdoor cat for far too long. You might feel differently. If you decide to go the agent route, I wish you the best of luck.

CHAPTER 12

Marketing

Marketing begins before the book is even released. Assuming you have a terrific story, the next steps are to get a good cover, set a competitive price, have a great book description, and pick the right title. If your book is being published traditionally, these details will be covered by your publisher, but if you're self-publishing it's all on you.

A Good Cover

A good cover tells the reader immediately what kind of book it is. You can test this by showing your cover to other people to get their take on it. If you wrote a mystery and someone says it looks like a romance, you're in trouble.

Compare your cover to books in the same category. Look at the popular books and take note of the font, placement, and size of the title. Your cover should look good thumbnail size because that's how potential readers may first view it. It shouldn't look amateurish or scream self-published. I was able to get away with using my own photos with added text in 2009, but authors have upped their game, and many self-published covers are even better than those put out by big publishing houses.

I can't stress this enough—a cover can make or break a book. You don't want to show up for the job interview as the shabbily dressed guy among a bunch of sharp-dressed men.

Set a Competitive Price

A competitive price is whatever the reader is willing to pay. At one time ninety-nine cents was a surefire way to get a ton of sales, and then the market was flooded with ebooks at that price point. Many of those books were not ready for prime time, and with that came the perception that a low price meant a bad book.

The good thing about self-publishing is the ability to make changes on the fly. See what comparable books are doing and what works for them, then make your own pricing decision accordingly.

My Method for Writing a Book Description

For sales purposes, a description has to convey the type of book, give a summary of the story, and entice the reader into buying or at least sampling your book.

The description also needs to be a certain length. Too long and you lose the reader. Too short and there's just not enough there. Readers who browse on Amazon.com or the Barnes & Noble site are used to seeing descriptions that take up a certain amount of space on the page. If your description doesn't fall within those parameters, it will just look "wrong." People make snap judgments and don't even know why sometimes. If you play by the rules, you won't give them a reason to bypass your book.

It's interesting to me that some of the best writers seem incapable of coming up with a suitable description of their own book. They're too close to the material and too emotionally invested. As usual, I have an opinion on the subject and my own personal method for crafting a description. My method's not the only way to go about it, of course, but it could be a good starting point for someone who is stuck.

When I do workshops, I illustrate my method using the publishers' descriptions of two popular books.

The Da Vinci Code by Dan Brown

Robert Langdon is a Harvard professor of symbology who can't stay out of trouble. Last seen in *Angels and Demons* (2000), this mild-mannered academic finds himself entangled in a deadly conspiracy that stretches back centuries. Visiting Paris on business, he is awakened at 2:00 a.m. by a call from the police: An elderly curator has been murdered inside the Louvre, and a baffling cipher has been found near the body. Aided by the victim's cryptologist granddaughter, Langdon begins a danger-filled quest for the culprit; but the deeper he searches, the more he becomes convinced that long-festering conspiracies hold the answer to the art lover's death.

Harry Potter and the Sorcerer's Stone by J. K. Rowling

Orphaned as a baby, Harry Potter has spent eleven awful years living with his mean aunt, uncle, and cousin Dudley. But everything changes for Harry when an owl delivers a mysterious letter inviting him to attend a school for wizards. At this special school, Harry finds friends, aerial sports, and magic in everything from classes to meals, as well as a great destiny that's been waiting for him...if Harry can survive the encounter. From an author who has compared to C. S. Lewis and Roald Dahl, this enchanting, funny debut novel won England's National Book Award and the prestigious Smarties Prize.

They're very different books, and at first glance, the descriptions don't seem to have much in common. But look closer, and (aha!) you'll notice a pattern, one you can use in describing your own book.

The first sentence of each starts with the main character and touches on his "ordinary world." We see that, like so many people we know, Robert Langdon is a Harvard professor of symbology, while poor Harry has spent eleven awful years living with hateful relatives.

Once the main character and his current situation are established, we learn that something changes. In Robert's case we find out that while he's visiting Paris on business, he is awakened at 2:00 a.m. by a call from the police: An elderly curator has been murdered inside the Louvre, and a baffling cipher has been found near the body. Harry, meanwhile, is just going along living his horrible life when suddenly an owl delivers a mysterious letter inviting him to attend a school for wizards.

I'm not sure about you, but in both cases, I'm definitely intrigued.

What happens next, you ask? Each description goes on to tell the reader a smattering of details so we get a feel for the type of story it is, but, and this is important, it really doesn't reveal much at all in the way of specifics. We learn that Robert begins a danger-filled quest for the culprit, but the deeper he searches, the more he becomes convinced that long-festering conspiracies hold the answer to the art lover's death.

Back at Hogwarts, Harry finds friends, aerial sports, and magic in everything from classes to meals, as well as a great destiny that's been waiting for him. For both novels the description only hints at what is to come. The reason it's not clearly spelled out? They want you to buy and read the book.

The Harry Potter book description adds one more thing at the end: hype. Awards are mentioned and comparisons to other authors are made. The book is called an enchanting, funny debut novel. The publisher wrote the hype. If you self-publish, you are now the publisher. Don't be afraid to mention awards won. Compare yourself to other authors if that's appropriate. Add a little tagline praising the book if you want.

When I self-published *A Scattered Life,* I impulsively added a line at the end of my description, something about the story being heartwarming and bittersweet and staying with the reader long after the last page was turned (ironic since it was a Kindle book and there weren't technically any pages). A friend who read the tagline said, "Oh, that was such a nice thing for them to say," and I was too embarrassed to tell her that there was no "them," it was only me.

Honestly? I couldn't really gauge how long the story would stay with the reader. And "long after the last page is turned," is not a precise length of time. I was told by early readers that the book stayed with them, and I hoped that would be the experience for other people as well.

Something to remember: specific nouns and strong verbs are your friends when you're writing a book description. *The Da Vinci Code* uses the following words and phrases:

trouble
entangled
deadly conspiracy
elderly curator
murdered
baffling cipher
danger-filled quest
culprit
long-festering conspiracies
death

Here are some from *Harry Potter and the Sorcerer's Stone*:

orphaned
owl delivers
mysterious letter
school for wizards
aerial sports
magic
great destiny

And another thing—try not to make the book or your characters sound depressing.

Depressing and sad are the kiss of death when you're trying to attract readers. But what about Nicholas Sparks, you say? His books make readers sob and people love them! True, but read the descriptions of his novels and see how the spin masters work their magic. These kinds of words and phrases are used:

sweet bond
magical healing
triumphant romance
tough truth
a dilemma
whopper of a secret

And from some other sad books:

emotional healing
brings the family together
triumph in the face of unspeakable tragedy

Hope is a good thing in fiction. Redemption too. What we don't usually seek out in a reading experience is pain all by itself. Just something to keep in mind.

So, to wrap things up, this is my way of writing book descriptions in a nutshell:

1) Establish the main character and his current situation.
2) Tell about the change (or the happening, or what have you).

3) Allude to what happens next in vague, but exciting terms.
4) Don't be afraid of hype.
5) Use strong verbs and specific nouns.

If you follow the formula and keep the length right, you should do fine.

Pick the Right Title

Titles can be tricky. For *The Long Way Home*, my original title was *The Road Trip*. My editor, Terry, asked if I'd rethink it after one of his colleagues assumed it would be a wild story à la the movie *The Hangover*. Argh! Really?

I liked my title, but I didn't want to give anyone the wrong impression. Terry suggested we put it to the test by posting four different titles on Amazon's Facebook page and letting people vote. I watched the page anxiously that day, and when the results came in I had to admit I'd been wrong. Sadly, *The Road Trip* didn't do well, and neither did Terry's suggestion, *The Possibility of Flying*. *The Long Way Home* was the winner by a lot.

Even knowing this, there are times I wish it were called *The Road Trip*. Feel free to use that title if you'd like.

Titles should be memorable, and ideally they should give an indication of what type of book it is. Run a few possibilities past your friends and family before you make the final decision. It's easy for us as writers to get attached to a title without realizing how it comes off to others.

CHAPTER **13**

When Your Family Doesn't Read Your Books

I once wrote a blog entry with this title, and the comments section blew up with writers saying that they couldn't get their family to read their writing for anything. Frankly, it's puzzling to us writers. If someone in my family wrote a novel, I'd be all over that puppy. I really believe that reading someone's writing is a glimpse into their soul, so to speak. And since I'm incredibly nosy, I'd welcome a chance to have that glimpse.

My mom and my sister Kay have read every book I've ever written, but that isn't the case for my immediate family.

My husband has read every word of my nonfiction, including interviews, but he hasn't read any of my fiction. In all fairness, I can count on one hand the number of novels I've seen him read in all the years I've known him. The books he's chosen in the past are nothing like the books I write. I'll admit it—I'm no Tom Clancy or John Grisham.

My older son, Charlie, proofreads some of my manuscripts; my youngest, Jack, gives me suggestions for plot points; my daughter, Maria, has been helpful in talking through fictional scenarios when I'm stuck. Each one has read a few of my novels. Some of my books just don't appeal to them, and I completely understand.

I've heard that Stephen King's wife is his first and ideal reader for all of his novels. That seems to be a successful arrangement. In an interview, author Christina Schwarz said her husband reads and critiques every word of her novels. I'm pretty sure I wouldn't like that, but it works for them.

Most of the writers who left comments on my blog had come to terms with the fact their family didn't read their books. Our families, after all, aren't usually our target audience. If they're supportive, that's huge. As for me, if my kids and husband prefer not to read them, I don't want them to do it just to please me.

CHAPTER 14

Writers' Insomnia—It's a Real Thing

Writer insomnia. Once you start writing novels, it's likely to happen. Personally I find it easy to fall asleep, but hard to stay asleep. I often wake up in the middle of the night with my mind whirring with story ideas or lists of writing-related tasks. I'm tired but wide awake. Ack. Talk about aggravating.

I used to blame lack of exercise, which makes sense, somewhat. Writing is only a notch above watching television as far as energy expended. But I've noticed that other sedentary people sleep just fine. Not only that, but when I do have active days, I still have sleep interruptions.

Another writer I know has a theory about this. Writers, he said, spend so much time in the equivalent of a dream state that our bodies think we've already slept a good many hours.

So then, when we do sleep, it seems excessive. His idea sounds logical to me. Sometimes after a particularly fruitful writing session, I do feel like I've awoken from a dream.

Some time ago, a story idea came to me during one of my middle-of-the-night sessions. I saw it clearly in my mind. There was a guy, a teenager, who couldn't sleep, so he began to go out walking after his parents had turned in for the night.

The story started out like this: I couldn't believe it was happening again. Couldn't sleep, couldn't sleep, couldn't sleep. It was a Monday night; school started the next day at 7:20 a.m., and I was exhausted, but my body didn't care. I shifted in bed and punched my pillow into different shapes, like that would help, even though it never did before.

I knew my character would witness something amazing during one of his nighttime walks, and he did, but even I was surprised at how the plot unfolded. Turned out my main character, Russ Becker, saw a strange astronomical event and then later found out that he had superpowers. The book became *Edgewood*, the first book in the series I mentioned earlier.

The *Edgewood* books are favorites of mine and I can thank writer insomnia for the inspiration, and my subconscious for putting the idea into story form. Now when I wake up in the middle of the night, I don't fight it. I just get up and make lists, read, or get some writing done. Because you never know when the ideas keeping you awake might just turn into something more.

CHAPTER 15

Making a Career as a Novelist

If you want to write books for a living, it's probably best not to follow my example. I've written women's fiction and books for middle-grade readers and young adults. And now this non-fiction writing book. Most of my fictional titles have elements of the supernatural, but four of them do not. If you look at the covers of my books, they are not branded in a way that is readily identifiable.

My son Charlie once had someone at work ask what kind of books his mother wrote. His answer? "Whatever she wants, really." This response delighted me because it portrayed me as a writer who follows her creative instincts rather than one who failed to plan.

My choices haven't always been the smartest, but I'm not complaining. I write the books I want to write, and it's turned out fine. It would have been better financially, though, if I'd stuck to one genre/age group and focused on that. From what I've observed, the indie authors who do the best tend to write series in popular genres and are brilliant at branding themselves. Check out the books of Bella Forrest, Russell Blake, and Claire Cook. At a glance you can tell what type of books they each write, and their covers are similar enough to look like siblings. They've all mastered branded marketing.

Me, I like to read different kinds of books, and I like to write different kinds of books as well. I follow the ideas. It's probably not the smartest business decision, but I'm happy with what I'm doing. If you're just starting out, you have the opportunity to mold your career from the get-go. You may find sticking to one genre to be advantageous.

Whether or not it feeds your soul is another matter.

CHAPTER 16

Reviews

If you've written a book, chances are someone is going to hate it. And they won't just hate it, they will despise it. They'll wonder how it ever got published and say the writing is amateurish and the main character, the one you modeled after yourself, is despicable and should be killed. It's enough to make a writer cry.

My favorite bad review said something like this: "This is the third book I've read by Karen McQuestion, and it's just as hokey and terrible as the last two." I wanted to leave a comment that said, *Stop reading them! There are millions of other books out there. Try some of those.* I didn't respond, though, because that would have been a big mistake. Reviewers are entitled to their opinion, even as I'm entitled to disagree. Putting my thoughts out there could potentially start a flame war, and what's to be gained from that? Frankly, I hate conflict, and I'd rather spend my time writing.

When a review starts out, "I wanted to like this book, I really did," I know I should duck, because a grenade is coming my way. Honestly, I have my doubts about them really wanting to like it, but I can't prove otherwise.

If a bad review has a valid point, keep that in mind for future books. If enough readers say the same thing, that's telling. Maybe you do wrap up your endings too quickly or fall short in describing characters. I've been accused of both and have adjusted accordingly.

Ignoring a bad review can be tough, I know. It stings. Try telling yourself that your book just isn't for them. And if that doesn't work, you might try looking up your favorite book and reading the posted one-star reviews. Even great books have haters. It helps to show that it's truly subjective. Another thing that helps is writing more books. I can shrug this kind of thing off more easily now that my numbers have increased.

The other problem with reviews is the lack thereof. How to get more reviews, you might wonder? I only know of one way, and that is to ask. Not your friends or family—your readers. I always leave a short note from the author (that would be me!) at the end of my novels saying that if you enjoyed the book, I'd love to read your thoughts in a review. It's true, it's not pushy, and it does make a difference. Try it and see for yourself.

CHAPTER 17

Why Isn't Anyone Buying My Book?

It's such torture to write a book and put it out in the world and then have it sit there doing nothing. Day after day with no sales at all. Refreshing the Amazon page over and over again does not change things. Believe me, I would know. I've written my fair share of books. Some have done remarkably well and some have sunk like a stone, and I wouldn't have been able to predict either of these outcomes ahead of time.

I have a theory about books that don't sell. I believe this happens for three reasons.

1) Your book is not as good as you think it is.

Ouch! I didn't mean to come off so harshly, but it's true that sometimes we are not the best judges of our novels. We created this fictional world. These characters are part of us, and we worked hard on this novel. It might take years before we can look back and see the cracks in the surface, if ever. Maybe this is our beginner novel, the one our someday masterpiece will be compared to with loving, forgiving eyes. How do you know if this is the case? If friends avoid talking about your book or say they've been meaning to read it but haven't gotten around to it yet, it's likely they tried it and didn't like it. I wouldn't take that as the last word on the subject, but it's something to think about.

2) It's a fabulous book with limited appeal.

If your novel's plot has, say, a heavy emphasis on fly-fishing, with lots of fabulous fly-fishing details, it might be a fly-fisherman's dream book. But maybe not so much for everyone else.

Or say you're a lifelong fan of the works of Charles Dickens, so you've written a novel in that style. It might be a little wordy in parts with tons of description and formal dialogue, just the way you intended. Don't be surprised if this doesn't work for most people. The right reader would love it, though. The challenge is to reach that reader.

3) It's a fabulous book with widespread appeal, but no one knows about it.

Now we're talking! Yes, you say, your book is fabulous, but obscure. How can people read a book they don't know about? They can't. You, my friend, have a visibility problem.

A lot of new authors make the mistake of trying to *sell* their book. They plaster social media with pushy messages: *Buy my book, buy my book, buy my book! Have you heard about my book? Hey, here's more about my book.*

Please stop. I can't get away fast enough.

Authors who do that are the equivalent of those guys at the mall who yell at you as you walk by. Ninety-nine percent of the time it does not work, and people find it irritating. Your goal is to make people *want* to buy your book.

Everyone thinks there's some marketing secret that other authors are keeping from them. If that's true, they haven't told me either. The things that work change as rapidly as the publishing world is changing. I started off posting on message boards, with my book links in my signature line. There are still places you can do this, but don't do it on the Amazon message boards. It is forbidden, and you will get flamed.

Book bloggers can be helpful in getting the word out, but they get deluged with requests, so ask respectfully and make sure your book matches up with their interests.

Some authors use book giveaways as a marketing tool either through their own social media sites, Amazon, or Goodreads. Others band together with other authors in their genre to do some cross-promotion.

Using your website to encourage readers to sign up for your newsletter is a great way to get the word out when you have giveaways or new releases. The only problem is that most people get way too much email as it is, so this is no small task. Making it easy for them helps. Be sure the sign-up box on your website is displayed prominently and that in each of your books you post a request politely asking readers to sign up. Provide them with a link. Those who loved your book will want to have the inside track on future books.

One idea is to think like a reader. If you were looking for your type of book, what would get you to buy it? A low price? A recommendation on a certain site? Word of mouth from a friend? If I were the writer who wrote the fly-fishing novel, I'd hang out on sites for fly-fishermen and never mention my book, but list it at the bottom in my signature line.

The most valuable suggestion I can give you is one that does not please most people. Do a little digging. Hang out at message boards and on social media and soak up the wisdom of other authors. My favorite is the Writer's Café at kboards.com. The writers there are smart, smart, smart (rule of three!), and they're generous to each other too. No one is as invested in your book as you are—put time and energy into finding different methods of getting the word out.

As the market changes, the way to reach readers changes too. Some paid advertising will work for a while and be less effective later on. Anything I mention about marketing here will be obsolete in a matter of months. You have to be adaptable and resourceful. What works for one writer may not work for you.

Keep trying and write another novel, because if someone reads your book and loves it, they'll go looking for more. One book feeds into another. Easier said than done, I know, but I can tell you with certainty that this is the one thing which worked for me.

And if you've already written one novel, you can do it again. Happy writing!

RECOMMENDED BOOKS

On Writing: A Memoir of the Craft, by Stephen King

The Writer's Journey: Mythic Structures for Writers, by Christopher Vogler

Save the Cat! The Last Book on Screenwriting You'll Ever Need, by Blake Snyder

Bird by Bird: Some Instructions on Writing and Life, by Anne Lamott

Killing the Top Ten Sacred Cows of Publishing, by Dean Wesley Smith

Take Off Your Pants!: Outline Your Books for Faster, Better Writing, by Libbie Hawker

RECOMMENDED MOVIES

Finding Forrester (Just for fun.)

Joseph Campbell: The Power of Myth (PBS series)

A Note from the Author

If after reading this book you go on to write your masterpiece, I wouldn't mind at all if you thanked me in the acknowledgments.

If you've enjoyed this book, I'd love to read your thoughts in a review. Really I would!

And to be notified of new releases and special giveaways, sign up to be one of my Elite Readers via my website: www.karenmcquestion.com. I would appreciate it. I promise not to spam you or share your email address.

Thank you!

Acknowledgments

I am grateful to the following people for their help with this book: Kay Ehlers, Geri Erickson, Jessica Fogleman, and Charlie McQuestion. I couldn't have done it without you!

I'd also like to thank every reader, blogger, librarian, author, and writing instructor who helped and encouraged me along the way. Your numbers are legion, but the names Alice L. Kent, Debra Garrett Curtiss, Robert Vaughan, Felicity Librie, Mary Michela, Emily Lewis, Wrainbeau Willis, Vickie Coats, Brandon Wright, Shelly San Juan, Kay Bratt, Kate Danley, Barbara Taylor Sissel, Michelle Schrubbe, Jeannée Sacken, Geri Ahearn, Leslie Wright, Catherine Bonner, Paige Brasher, Tiffany Lovering, Gail Grenier Sweet, Maria Rollyson, Stacy Romanjuk, Delia Ephron, Danielle Urban, Lesley Kagen, Cyndy Salamati, Rex Kusler, Kristine Vetter, Judi Littlefield, Derya Remsi, Carolyn Parkhurst, Dorothy Svien, and Claire Cook come readily to mind. My apologies to those whose names I've omitted. Please know I hold you in my heart.

I'm also appreciative to the Hartland Public Library, and Jan Jensen and Nancy Massnick in particular, for hosting my novel-writing talk. The copious notes I took in preparation for that presentation were the genesis of this book.

Lastly, I'd like to thank my husband, Greg, and our three kids, Charlie, Maria, and Jack. Your support and love has meant the world to me.

ABOUT THE AUTHOR

Karen McQuestion writes books for kids, teens, and adults, and is published in print, ebook, and audio. All told, her books have sold over a million copies worldwide.

Many of her titles have spent time on the top 100 Kindle list. Her publishing story has been covered by the *Wall Street Journal, Entertainment Weekly*, and NPR. McQuestion has also appeared on ABC's *World News Now* and *America This Morning*. She lives in Hartland, Wisconsin.

Notes

Notes

Made in the USA
Monee, IL
17 May 2021

68746033R00085